like a
MOTHER

BIRTHING BUSINESSES, BABIES, AND A LIFE BEYOND LABELS

Published in Canada, for Global Distribution by YGTMedia Co. www.ygtmedia.co/publishing
To order additional copies of this book: publishing@ygtmedia.co

Edited by Tania Jane Moraes-Vaz and Kelly Lamb
Interior design and typesetting by Doris Chung
Cover design by Michelle Fairbanks
Author Photo by Helen Tansey Photography

TORONTO

Written with appreciation, backslaps, and high fives to my Mabel's Labels co-founders Cynthia Esp, Julie Ellis, and Tricia Mumby.

I have so much gratitude for my incredible mom, Ann Cole, who has been my number one supporter throughout my life.

Thankful for my women folk, mentors, cheerleaders, helpers, the Mabelhood community, and those who have always had my back during this journey.

And of course, so much love to the six best decisions I've ever made: Mack, Posy, Spencer, Jessamy, Clancy, and Finian. They have been very patient and supportive of their busy mama.

From the Cofounder of Mabel's Labels™

JULIE COLE

like a
MOTHER

BIRTHING BUSINESSES, BABIES,
AND A LIFE BEYOND LABELS

Table of Contents

Steering the Mothership

As women, we wear a lot of labels. Some were given to us at birth, some were earned through hard work, and some were gained from enduring the hard knocks of life. Others have evolved and changed along the way, just as we have. Some labels bring us joy and are a sense of pride, while others bring uncertainty and stress. Some of the labels I've worn throughout my life include daughter, sister, friend, student, lawyer, partner, mother, volunteer, entrepreneur, advocate, blogger, speaker, and CEO. And while they don't wholly define me, just as your labels don't truly sum up all that is you, they're a good starting point for me to tell my story, well, parts of my story. Life is complicated, and so are our lives.

Most of you will know me as the co-creator of Mabel's Labels. Others will know me as the mom to Mack, Posy, Spencer, Jessamy, Clancy, and Finian. Yes, six kids and a successful international business—I wasn't kidding around when I said life is complicated. It's also loud and busy! But life really is a wonderful ride that teaches us so much every day. I've realized along the way that sharing what I've learned and helping others makes it all so much more enjoyable.

One question I'm asked more than any other (even more than "Are all those kids yours?") is "How did a group of four young moms end up in a basement making labels while your kids slept?" Believe me, it's a destiny I never envisioned for myself. I was a lawyer and had my path all mapped out. But that's the funny thing about life, it rarely cares about your perfectly mapped out plans.

My journey into entrepreneurship really started when I realized that I wasn't willing to choose between juggling a demanding legal career and my growing family. I already had three kiddos in tow when my firstborn received an autism diagnosis at the tender age of three. I didn't know a lot about autism at the time, so I dove headfirst into discovering everything I could about it so I could do everything possible to help support Mack, while also being the mom I needed to Posy and Spencer, who were just babies. One thing I quickly realized was that I needed to pivot. My priorities changed—and I needed to change my plan as well.

The new path wasn't straight or freshly paved—it so rarely is—it was a bumpy ride through weeds at times, but along the way I was able to create something I was proud of, with, and for, my family. I wrote this book as a resource for you on all things about life, motherhood, and entrepreneurship because let's face it, one of these things is not like the other. Everything looks and feels different—even your mind operates differently the moment you become a mom. And I'm not just talking about feeling foggy and having "mombrain." For many of us, things change the moment we find out we're entering parenthood. New labels get attached to us, and finding and carving our own identity sometimes takes a backseat. I went from being "Ms. Cole" and "Julie" at work to being "Mack's mom" in the park. Every change, even the best ones, can cause you to catch your breath and feel the need to regroup.

Consider this book your mini guide and cheat sheet to life, motherhood, business, and everything in between! I can't guarantee that I'll teach you how to get your kids to pick up after themselves or instruct you on how to create a multimillion-dollar business in your basement, but I hope that my story inspires you, or at least answers some of your questions about how I did it. Like everyone, I'm still a work in progress. And in my life, the line between motherhood and business often gets blurred, although I do try to be present in whatever role I'm in at the moment. My book is set up that way as well. I've included mom, biz, and life hacks throughout to hopefully make your hectic life a little easier so you can operate #likeamother. I also shine a light for special needs children, especially those on the autism spectrum.

I hope my story shows you what is possible for you and your family. Love and success look different for everyone, and it goes beyond labels, so don't worry about those. As we say at Mabel's Labels: "Leave the labeling to us!"

Feel free to screenshot any of the mom/biz/life hacks and share and tag us along with your Mabelhood @mabelslabels @juliecoleinc and let us know which ones resonate the most with you.

More than anything, come say hi and connect with me and our team! We love hearing from you, and there is always room for a question or two, or even a quick connection!

chapter one

When Plans Change—Change with Them

Ever had all your plans go awry in one fell swoop? When you thought you were on one path only to discover that your itinerary was changed without your knowledge and you had to just go with it? That happened to me when I became a mother. I had heard the expression, "There is one beautiful baby in the world and every mother has it," and when my son Mack was born, I knew I had that baby. When my beautiful baby boy was diagnosed with autism, there began the life I hadn't bargained for.

My parenting philosophy changed entirely with the diagnosis. I had always imagined myself as a mother who would push for my son's individualism, supporting any direction his nature took him. But then, I had to change direction and work hard to make him "fit in" to be like other kids his age. He had things like *Transformers, Pokémon*, and *SpongeBob* shoved down his throat with the hope that it would help him connect with his peers. When we walked through toy stores, I'd watch what other little boys were begging their mothers for. When they'd drop to the ground in a temper tantrum, I'd step over their kicking feet to reach for that very item for my guy. If that was what "typical" boys desperately wanted, then that's what my boy would have.

After four years of undergraduate study, a two-year master's degree, three years of law school, and a year of articling, I imagined my credentials would land me a hot job in the hub and heart of a cool city. I could picture it before it happened: swanky suit, power lunches, lipstick dabbed to perfection, and a cell phone reminding me minute-by-minute just how important I was as I sashayed in my Manolo Blahnik heels into court!

Well, my life was nowhere close to *that* vision. That vision quickly turned into my measuring the success of a day by getting through it without smelling like baby pee or toddler vomit. The vision of Manolo Blahniks had transformed into the reality of my favorite pair of fuzzy bunny slippers. Oh, they were so much comfier than heels!

It didn't take me long to realize that a legal career did not particularly accommodate women with small children, especially children with special needs. This is not to say that I didn't have the opportunity to use my finely tuned legal skills—the definitions had just altered. "Advocacy" now meant being an expert on school board policies and understanding what rights the Education Act provided. I wrote to Members of Parliament, and I protested in the rain on the front lawn of our government offices for autism funding. And now, as a business-woman and a mother of six, my skills in negotiation are constantly put to the test!

There is a fantastic poem about life with a special needs child that was given to me when my son was first diagnosed. The poem—"Welcome to Holland" by Emily Perl Kingsley—compares having a child to planning a trip to Italy. You and all your friends are planning a trip to Italy, so you buy all the gear you'll need, learn some Italian, and make plans to visit the sights. Everyone is going to the same place and seeing the same things. Then you have a child with a disability and become separated from your friends, who made it to Italy and are touring the Colosseum. Instead, you find yourself in Holland. Now you have to learn a different language, become part of a different culture, and meet different people. But you see that Holland has tulips, windmills, and Rembrandts. It's not where you wanted to go, but you are there, and it's not so bad.

This is my way of telling you that when we have kids, there are no guarantees. I am not working in a swanky office downtown, but I am in Holland. Mack brought us here, and it's a place we love because we are here with him. It's not as glamorous as Rome, but we couldn't have imagined being anywhere else.

The analogy also applies to life in general. So often our best-laid plans end up going awry. In parenthood and in business, you have to adapt, pivot, learn, and move forward. I always thought I'd be a family law lawyer, but I ended up having a family, which required me to be flexible and fully present. I teamed up with my sister and two close friends, who were also new moms. We wanted to create a business that would fill a need we encountered as moms, which also allowed us to provide for our kiddos.

They say starting a business is not for the faint of heart, nor is it for everyone. I've realized that some entrepreneurs are born, and some become entrepreneurs out of necessity. Well, I fall into the latter category. My circumstances and son's autism diagnosis threw me head first into finding a solution that would allow me to care for him and provide him with the support he needed to thrive while figuring out a way to still bring in income.

You're likely wondering how a lawyer, a teacher, a printing manager, and a financial planner connected and created Mabel's Labels. In our case, it was luck. My sister, Cynthia Esp, and our two friends, Julie Ellis and Tricia Mumby, got along really well, and we eventually became family; after university, one married our brother, and the other married our young uncle. So friends turned into family turned into business partners. I don't always recommend going into business with friends or loved ones, unless you have a clear understanding of each other and clearly outlined boundaries. And in our case, we clicked. Our personalities had great synergy; so did our skill sets.

In those early days, having four partners contributed to our early growth. With four brains at the table and sets of feet on the street, we could be highly productive. Although we were busy with small children and day jobs, a partnership of four allowed us to divide and conquer. I often see solo entrepreneur friends having to do everything on their own and realize that while there are challenges with a partnership of four, there are many benefits, particularly when starting out.

In additon to being able to divide up the work, we could also be there for each other when support was needed. If someone had a sick child or was about to deliver another baby, the other three were there to pitch in. When one of us had doubts about the business and wondered what we got ourselves into, the three others could talk her off the ledge.

Do your research

Before we launched Mabel's Labels, there was a lot of research and development that had to happen. We tested countless kinds of material and had labels stuck on cups and sitting in our dishwashers for months on end. We knew we needed to create a product that WE would love. As moms ourselves, we knew our customers would want their labels to be extremely durable, highly personalized, and beautiful. We chose a name that was cute and easy to remember, Mabel, and gave us the opportunity to create a playful and unique brand.

From the very beginning, we took our branding and design very seriously. Finding the right material was one challenge, but the next was setting up our website. They were the early days of e-commerce and without a computer nerd among us, we needed to figure out how to navigate the world of online shopping.

Luckily, like most women entrepreneurs, we were savvy socially and not afraid to reach out to experts and friends to ask questions and for favors. We firmly believed in the idea that there are no stupid questions and did not let ego or pride get in the way of us getting this business going. We tapped into many resources early on, including some of our very clever IT friends from our university days. We were not sure how we were going to pay to have our website developed, but we found a solution with our old university pals. We needed a website, and they wanted a foosball table. THAT we could pitch in and afford. Yes, the first website for Mabel's Labels was built in exchange for a foosball table.

Once we had all our equipment ready to go in my sister's dingy basement—yes, that's the reality of starting a business—it was time for us to spread the word and let the world know that Mabel's Labels was born. With a budget of $100—and in the days before social media—we had to get creative. Again, we called on our friends. We bought stamps and wrote letters to everyone we knew with a flyer begging them to buy our labels and to tell their friends about Mabel's Labels. Talk about real grassroots, organic marketing. We licked those stamps, mailed those letters, and then waited. I wrote to every media outlet with the hope that one would be interested in our story. After all, a few moms were trying to build a label empire from a basement during nap times and nursery school.

And that's exactly what we did. Moms CAN build businesses after bedtime and create business plans during playdates.

Leave it to trusty moms to spread the word, and spread they did. We did production in the early days two nights a week. Often, kids would be put to bed and we'd start production at 8:00 p.m. Sometimes we were there making labels until 2:00 a.m., only to get up at 6:00 a.m. to take care of children or do daycare drop-offs and head to day jobs. They were not glamorous days. Even less glamorous was our work environment. My sister had a very modest house in downtown Hamilton, a city southwest of Toronto, Ontario. Things were pretty cozy for us in the basement. On hot nights, we would open the basement door leading outside to get fresh air through our makeshift production facility. It wasn't uncommon for stray cats to wander in and check in on our label-making activities. Usually, one of the partners was tasked each evening with shooing the stray cats out of the basement.

It wasn't long before we needed a bit of help. Fortunately, we had a cousin who was home from university and stepped up to help us during the summer. Looking back, I have no idea how we would have made it through that summer without her. Those were early days, and we didn't completely know our cycle. We were only just learning that summer meant "back-to-school" season, and to date, it is still the busiest time of year for us. When our cousin returned to university in the fall, we had to hire our first "stranger." Before that, everyone who helped was one of our moms, aunts, siblings, or friends. We called them our Mabelhood. We had a girls' getaway weekend at the cottage where our friends spent the entire time stamping flyers for us. We paid them in wine and fun stories.

Once we hired "real" employees, it suddenly occurred to us that maybe the basement was not the best environment for our staff. We were not entirely sure the conditions were even legal. We knew it was time to upgrade, but being a little cautious, we didn't want to invest in commercial real estate. We were a new business, and we didn't want to get ahead of ourselves and create debt when we didn't really know if we could afford that rent.

As such, we suggested that my sister buy a bigger house with a bigger basement, and that is exactly what she did! For all of us, finances were very tight, but Mabel's Labels could afford to pay some rent to my sister, which helped in her purchase of our next Mabel's Labels headquarters on Aberdeen Avenue. When we moved in there, we could not believe how spacious it was, and we imagined being there for five years. Within two years, it was full of equipment and many more bodies. One of our early employees still remembers walking into our Aberdeen office on her first day of work and seeing me sitting on the floor with my laptop. She laughed, wondering why a co-founder didn't even have a desk to sit at. That gives you some idea of how tight we became for space. We were bursting at the seams, and it was time to take the plunge and rent a commercial space. That was in 2008, and today, we're still in that 14,000-square foot production facility and offices in Hamilton.

Sometimes your circumstances will lead you toward your next goal, your next destination. Stay open to it. It won't always look like how you planned—I mean, hello, I thought I would be changing the world of family law, and here I am, co-founder of a multimillion-dollar label company that brings joy to parents and kids alike! Sometimes Italy ends up being Holland, different but great. Yeah, I'll take this plan any day over the one I originally charted for myself. Stay curious to where your life leads you. Your children may just help you chart a new course.

#bizhack

Trying to find that business idea? Go through your day and find something that annoys you. Is there something you could make better? Or prettier? That might be your business idea. Find a pain point and take that pain away.

#lifehack

"You can't get to courage without rumbling with vulnerability." –Brené Brown

#momhack

Never underestimate the power of your Mabelhood community. Lean on them. Call on them for support. Word spreads like wildfire, and before you know it, there is a mama there for whatever it is you need.

chapter two

Focus on the Important Things

I remember when we first started Mabel's Labels in 2003, so many people thought we were ridiculous to leave our comfy, cushy, "secure" careers to start something that had no guarantees of succeeding. Secretly, though, I knew that we would win with Mabel's Labels, because we knew that we had a great idea, and we had put in the time and research to do it properly. We also really believed we had the best product for parents who were done trying to label their kids' things with masking tape or permanent marker.

When you step out of the traditional workforce and pursue the life of entrepreneurship, people WILL think you are crazy, and they will have no problem sharing that with you. It's true. Starting a business is not a life for the risk adverse. A healthy appetite for risk is definitely a requirement. Because it takes a toll—on your family, on your relationships, on you. You gotta be able to withstand the heat.

The best reaction came from our grandpa. He greatly valued financial security and seeing four highly educated young women leaving good careers was incomprehensible to him. However, it wasn't long before he was on board with Mabel's Labels and bragging to all the old ladies at his bridge club about our adventure.

Some people understood the idea of a few moms doing a "side hustle" for a little extra grocery money, and we certainly are considered the pioneers of the "mompreneur" movement. It's a term that gained a lot of momentum but then fell out of favor. I understand why it did—we are entrepreneurs, and our mom status doesn't need to be included. There go the labels again, right?! And "mompreneur" is one label I don't like to wear because it is gendered and comes with a sense that we're not serious about business. For some, the word conjures up images of a mom who loves knitting and sells some of her work in between PTA meetings and dropping kids off at hockey. Nope. Not us.

I certainly wasn't a label-making hobbyist. In fact, I'd never made a label before in my life. Also, we took the business very seriously from the start. We had a business plan, took minutes at our meetings, and managed our budgets. We treated it like a business because it was. We knew it was go big or go home from day one. Not making this work was not an option. These were not the actions of women who were not thinking big. However, the word "mompreneur" felt relatable to me for a few reasons. First, it was a business that was started as a direct result of my being a mother. If I didn't have children, I would have never known there was a need. If I had not gone through my son's diagnosis, I would not have been inspired to start a business. And truthfully, I really was building a business between playdates and during nap times. Like the term or not, it was one that applied to us, and we were seen as some of the originals. It played out well from a public relations perspective because our story was a fun one and our implied lifestyle was very appealing to many young moms.

But like we say with many titles: if you don't like them, leave the labeling to us.

We've all had that experience of dealing with naysayers or "trolls" in our lives. There are a few things that always help me through any negativity or shade that gets thrown my way. First, I consider the source. Is it someone I know, love, and respect? Is it someone who loves me and wants the best for me? If so, then I will entertain their concerns. A random stranger? A jealous old "friend" or someone on the internet who is hiding behind an anonymous profile? They get zero airtime. I also remind myself of a great Babe Ruth quote: "The loudest boos always come from the cheapest seats."

I think it's important to also note the people who are not clapping when you're winning. They are the people who are not on your team. So, with naysayers and negativity about your dreams, really consider whose opinions matter. Whose life is it anyway?

There will always be people who assign you titles, roles, and labels.

Who project their opinions, limitations, and more onto you. It's not your job to like them or to please them. Your job is to stay true to you, to your mission, to your vision, to your why, and to keep going. Let your success be what motivates you, not their negative opinions. They will always wonder how you will do it until you actually accomplish it. So keep going and take whatever it is that you pour your time, energy, and resources into seriously from day one.

Your why is important

Having a clear vision of why you are starting your endeavor also helps you stay focused from the onset. When we created Mabel's Labels almost two decades ago, there were two important *whys* that led to the launch of our business.

The first reason was to fill the need that the four of us noticed in the marketplace. As moms, we learned firsthand that makeshift labels of tape and markers weren't cutting it. They were ugly, and they weren't doing the job.

The second reason was the true catalyst for me. Mack's diagnosis shifted everything for me and my family, and I needed a work environment that provided some flexibility so I could dedicate time to focus on my son's therapy and advocating for him. Entrepreneurship was the answer.

Taking the leap into entrepreneurship was daunting. Even though the four of us were intelligent, educated, and willing to put in the work, we lacked certain tools. We didn't have a business degree or any entrepreneurial experience, but we were dedicated to taking the steps necessary. We found mentors and asked questions of every entrepreneur and businessperson we encountered. We set up a business plan, put together a Shareholders Agreement, and protected our trademark and copyright. We knew we wanted to create a top quality product and brand, and we took our time to get it right.

Know your market

Our market is moms. And being moms ourselves, we know our market well. Moms want to feel connected to the brands they support and that word of mouth is KING in the mom market. We moms talk about products we love like it is a full-time job. We knew that if we could create a product loved by moms, they would take care of our marketing by telling their friends about us.

Imagine our delight when social media finally arrived. That meant moms could now bring word of mouth online, and our marketing really took off. Moms began telling their communities about us on their blogs, sharing their labels on their Facebook pages, and sharing photos on Instagram. We started doing blogger outreach well before most other brands. We created "The Mabelhood," an online community where we provide our customers with top-notch content. It's no surprise that we have over 200,000 Facebook fans. Knowing our market allowed us to reach them in the ways they wanted to be reached.

KNOW YOUR CORE VALUES

Much like how your family core values or personal core values are important, I believe these also fall into business as well. Your business is an extension of you—your brand, your personality, your ethos. We were only a few years into Mabel's Labels when we realized the importance of creating and *committing* to our core values. As entrepreneurs, we were in the unique position to establish a company culture that we believed in. We could create the dream culture that we all desired. The wheels began to turn. We got to work and really began digging into what was at the core of our company. It was a lengthy process, including interviewing staff members, customers, and co-founders alike. Since established, our core values have guided us through many difficult times and decisions that needed to be made. They help us stay true to our voice and to our brand promise in all of our interactions, products, and relationships. Think of your core values as the heartbeat or the compass of your business. They will inform you when you are operating in misalignment or are not in integrity. They say your customers are the lifeline of your business. True. But in my opinion, your core values are the arteries that connect your business to your clients and customers alike. They are what keeps your business thriving and flourishing at the end of the day.

We have learned many benefits and lessons around core values, including never compromising on them. This can be difficult—there are distractions and temptations along the way. I distinctly remember a very high-profile brand that wanted to do a partnership with us. From a marketing perspective, this would have been extremely beneficial for us. There was one issue: this incredible company conducted themselves in a way that did not align with our core values. We declined partnering with them, and you can imagine their shock. They flew from their head office to our humble headquarters to try to understand our decision and convince us it would be okay.

We turned to our core values and of course, like the trusty compass they are, they told us that this organization was not a fit. Was it difficult to commit to our core values with an opportunity to make money staring at us? Sort of. Heck, we like making money, and I think the marketing team all cried a little that day. But our core values made the decision for us. In the end, we learned that by not compromising, bigger and better opportunities knock, and without risking customer loyalty and trust. We were not about to risk losing the brand we worked so hard to build. Trust and loyalty is difficult to create in your customers, and can be lost in an instant. So take time to cultivate it and nurture it continuously.

The lesson we learned, and one I have shared many times with other entrepreneurs and influencers was this: If you pass up on the opportunities that don't align with your core values, better opportunities will follow. If you compromise on your core values and work with partners that don't align with your brand, you will damage it beyond repair, and companies you want to work with will not pursue you. Always wait for the right fit.

Companies who are committed to their core values do more than throw good intentions on a sign and post it in the office lunchroom. They are not lip service. Core values are integrated into everything—your hiring practices, your policies, your interactions with customers and with each other. You create interview questions that integrate what is important to your company so that you make good hires. Many people can be trained to do a particular job, but they can't be trained to be a culture fit.

Core values help with decision-making. If you are having a difficult time making a decision in your business, turn to your core values. They will guide you!

I want to take you through a series of two case studies where our core values were put into action, to give you an idea of how it helped guide our decision-making and next steps.

CORE VALUE 1: RESPECT EVERY INDIVIDUAL

We thought a lot about what that means. That statement was way too generic and wide. So we needed to put it into practice. One way to do this over the years has been through our approach to inclusivity when it comes to people living with disabilities. I occasionally share the Mabel's Labels approach with a governmental body that spreads awareness and tries to increase employment for people with disabilities.

I suppose for us, this kind of inclusivity came very naturally. We have an aunt who has an intellectual disability and loved working at Mabel's Labels for many years collecting coffee mugs, tidying the kitchen, shredding paper, and chatting with everyone at the office. She knew more of what was happening at the office than I did. Although she recently retired, her involvement gave our entire staff a peek into the value people with disabilities can bring to a work environment. We are inclusive in our hiring practices, how our office is set up, and how we honor our team.

Diversity is good for everyone. We have enjoyed many different personalities and abilities that make our workplace exciting and fun. How boring it would be if we were all the same! I have found that some of our employees who are neuro-diverse are exceptionally loyal, staying with us for years or returning every year for our busy seasons. It may at times take a little bit longer to train these employees, but be patient because you'll reap the benefits. Our team members have been diligent, loyal, and highly productive.

This core value challenged us to question our assumptions about this population. We had assumed that these team members would be slow but steady in completing their tasks. Eventually on the production floor, we had technology-collected data reporting on how productive each pack line team member was. To our surprise, two of our team members who identify as neuro-diverse were among the most productive in the facility. One broke record after record.

Sometimes being inclusive means that you must collaborate and communicate with agencies, which can take up time. Our experience is that it is a good investment—everyone is on the same team and wants to see the employee succeed AND the business succeed. This is just one example of how to integrate this core value into your business.

CORE VALUE 2: FOCUS ON RESULTS

While most companies clocked hours and had a mandatory attendance policy unless you were sick or had a legit emergency, we, for many years, operated as a Results Only Work Environment, otherwise known as ROWE™. Today, while not in a formal ROWE™, we have always focused on results rather than just presenteeism.

Being results focused allows us to witness our staff achieving their goals instead of concerning ourselves with how or where they are spending their time. It measures employees' value not by how many hours they are seen at the office or how long they sit at their desk. Each employee, together with their manager, develops clear and measurable job expectations. Employees are given the autonomy to achieve outcomes in the most productive way possible so each person has control over how they spend their time to effectively get the job done. There's more flexibility, and the focus shifts from putting in time to ensuring excellent service.

Mabel's Labels started because the founders had the desire to leave the traditional workforce, which felt broken and unaccommodating to people, particularly mothers, who wanted to raise their families while having fulfilling careers and lives. We also had the desire to not micromanage adults and watch what time they were arriving to and leaving the office. Judging performance by how many hours they were present in an office didn't seem effective and counterintuitive to how we, ourselves, worked and were productive. In short, we wanted to treat adults like adults. It was no surprise that when you treat staff members like adults, they act like adults.

We noticed immediately that team members no longer policed each other. They no longer wasted their time looking at the clock to see what their colleagues were doing or if they were coming in on time. When coworkers are babysitting each other and noticing when people come and go, it can create a culture of "sludge." ROWE™ defines sludge as those little comments of judgment that bring down your coworkers and hurt the work environment. Imagine a mom gets her kid ready for daycare. On the way to drop-off, the kiddo gets sick, so mom has to turn around and get them cleaned up. She's then tasked with finding alternative daycare. If she's lucky, a mom or friend can take her child for the day. Mom finally arrives at work half an hour late, and a coworker peers up from her laptop and says, "Nice of you to join us." That is sludge. And it leaves you feeling exhausted and defeated. Quite simply, we wanted to make sure that everyone was too busy managing their own goals. Staff would no longer keep tabs on anyone else's business or gossip about the attendance records of their colleagues. That, in itself, contributed to a positive work environment.

People also became extremely transparent and honest. A parent didn't have to pretend they were sick in order to attend their child's Christmas Concert at school. They could attend and then share the pictures with us at work the next day or post them on their social media accounts without fear of being "caught." There WAS no getting "caught." Unfortunately, women are still carrying the emotional, mental, and physical load of parenthood. Households are not yet being run democratically. And this is not just moms; women, in general, are doing a lot of caregiving for elder relatives, pets, neighbors, and friend's children.

Productivity increased because staff didn't have to hide behind presenteeism. We accomplished a lower rate of absenteeism, decreased use of medical benefits, and employee performance ratings went up. Offering this kind of work environment helped us attract great employees and set us apart from competing employers.

In our first year in a ROWE™, we had a great year in sales! The question we're asked the most about this way of operating is if ROWE™ isn't working for a few people, do you take it away altogether? Quite simply, no. We don't. If an employee can't manage their goals, they aren't a great fit with the company and we part ways.

Being focused on results is difficult if the leadership in a company is not ready to commit to results and hold people accountable. Some leaders aren't comfortable with that and find it easier to focus on office hours, FaceTime, and physical presence. Not every business is ready to focus on results.

A case study

We dove into the unknown when one of our young and adventurous IT team members decided to work from Europe for two months. We went into this situation knowing it would be the ultimate ROWE™ experiment. Our IT team member understood that if his goals were not being met from whatever youth hostel he was hanging out in, he'd have to catch the first flight home if he wanted to keep his job.

And how did this experiment turn out? Highly successful, actually. He delivered to his team, met project deadlines, and communicated regularly with other departments and managers. And he accomplished all of this by working creatively and effectively.

Here are some of the things he learned from this adventure:

- Early on, he found that it was difficult to find the time to plan his travels and see what he wanted to see while working full time. He solved this problem by hiring a travel consultant to organize his itinerary. This allowed him to focus on getting his work done while also visiting the places he wanted to go.

- He discovered that Wi-Fi connections and the working atmosphere at fast food restaurants and coffee shops were not up to snuff. He turned to Google and found www.sharedesk.net. With it, he was able to find coworking space.

- In various cities, he rented office space where he had access to a reliable internet connection. This allowed him to get down to business. Once he was done, he was free to go off on another adventure.

- In many European cities, he found other IT professionals and connected with them, sharing his work and ideas. Connections and inspiration are greatly valued at Mabel's Labels.

- He had the opportunity to attend trade shows in cities

throughout Europe that he would have not otherwise been able to attend. ROWE™ allowed for this "out of the box" professional development.

The most valuable ROWE™ lesson we learned through this experience is that there are opportunities for team members to follow their passion. There is no reason why a committed employee who has a strong sense of their professional goals can't achieve results while fulfilling other lifelong dreams.

Whatever your core values within your business, don't be afraid to commit to them and implement them, especially when the going gets tough. When you focus on work ethic, results, skill over other markers such as clocking in and out or days present vs. out of office, you give your team members the opportunity to step up and bring their whole selves to your mission and vision. And when you have your entire team aligned with your vision, that is how you grow and scale at hyper speed. Together you go far, faster!

We create a great work culture

At Mabel's Labels, living by our core values has always been a passion. We understand what we are not willing to waiver on, and we will hire and fire by these core values. It allows us to practice our business with pride and also helps with decision-making.

When we hire people, we make sure to get the right people on the bus. We can train people to do their jobs, but we need to know that they are going to fit with our culture and share our core values. As such, we learned to hire slow and fire fast. If someone is not a fit for your company, do not keep them. They will impact morale, and you are not doing them any favors. They will find what they are passionate about, but they need to be moved along if it is not working out.

We put people first

I have always believed that your network is your net worth. In the early days, we tapped into the expertise of everyone we knew. I still attend regular networking events and am a part of several online entrepreneurial support groups. I have a mentor and I am a mentor. We treat our customers exactly how they should be treated—like our company can't exist without them. As such, we have loyalty programs, brand ambassadors, and are constantly exceeding our customers' expectations.

Is your family prepared?

People always ask what my biggest regret is and I honestly don't have one. There are no mistakes, only lessons—and we certainly have learned our share along the way. I would urge people thinking of starting a business to consider how it will affect your family.

When people start a business, they imagine what it will look like. It includes visions of inspiration, innovation, entrepreneurial thinking, fame, and a lot of money! That very sexy perspective is fairly inaccurate. When I was making labels in a dingy basement until 2:00 a.m. every morning, then getting up with kids at 6:00 a.m., reality set in quickly. I think our families must also be aware of what entrepreneurship actually looks like. If you have a partner or spouse, they really need to be 100 percent on board with your start-up. They must realize that you will be working constantly without any income for, potentially, years. It's best not to romanticize what the entrepreneurial life looks like.

Entrepreneurship and motherhood require you to keep going and keep anchoring into that strong, yet elusive WHY that might evade you some days especially if you are running on less than two hours of sleep for three days and counting, in your Herculean effort to do it all and do it well. Whatever your business journey looks like, know that you're never alone. Dig deep into your vision and remind yourself of why you started doing this in the first place.

#bizhack

It may sound clichéd, but make sure you love what you do. The more you love it, the more likely you are to be successful. Of course, we all have parts of our jobs that we don't like. But overall, you have to be happy with your work or business.

#lifehack

"The obligation for working mothers is a very precise one; the feeling that one ought to work as if one did not have children, while raising one's children as if one did not have a job." –Annabel Crabb

#momhack

Family meetings are a great way to ensure everyone has a voice. Start by opening with some positive things going on in the family. Talk about family goals and tasks, and make a plan on how to achieve them. Give everyone the chance to speak without interruption.

chapter three

Having It All

Have you ever asked yourself what having it all means to you? I know our society preaches a very idealistic and skewed version of what having it all really means. But who decides this? Since when did we outsource our life decisions to everyone else around us? I find that when it comes to women and entrepreneurship (heck, women in general), there's a very gendered notion or expectation. As a mom and entrepreneur, it often feels very much like society expects and projects that we could and should "have it all." And I am all for this, except it's unrealistic. It would leave many of us burned out, spinning our wheels out of sheer exhaustion. Oh wait, we're already doing this dance right now. And I long walked off that dance floor when I chose to start my business instead of choosing between going back to work or caring for my son.

I have reflected often at what this means—must I have a success-ful career, happy and thriving children, a fulfilling marriage, attend yoga regularly, have book club and wine nights with my girlfriends, while also being head of the PTA? Even writing that makes me feel exhausted! Can any one person do all those things? Who is to say those *things* will even make us happy? Who gets to define our happiness?

The one lesson I learned from having a large family and a business is that the notion of "having it all" means different things to different people.

For instance, I recall a cover of *Time* magazine with a couple lying leisurely on the beach. The title "The Childless Couple: When Having It All Means Not Having Children" proposed that "having it all" is attainable only by those who choose to forgo parenthood.

To say I found the cover—both the photo and words—disturbing on a few levels would be an understatement. Is this the way that "childless by choice" couples spend their time? I have many childless friends who do not pass their time lounging on beaches. Like most responsible adults, they have jobs, care for their elderly parents, are hands-on aunts and uncles, take care of pets, do volunteer work, maintain their homes, etc. The cover presented childless couples as self-indulgent and self-centered, which is an offensive and unfair stereotype that we need to move past.

I also wondered how this would make couples with fertility issues feel. My friends, who have had to deal with infertility, aren't lounging on beaches either. And they certainly don't feel like they "have it all."

Their time is spent at clinics having invasive procedures done. And those who have pursued adoption have had to jump through hoops and travel long and difficult roads to bring their children home. Hardly a day at the beach, if you ask me.

And what about parents? How did that cover make someone like me feel? It tells me I cannot have a full life because I chose to bring other people into it. Most parents, myself included, can't imagine life without their children. So the cover really deserved nothing more than an exasperated eye roll.

What does "having it all" mean anyway? I've heard it said that you can have it all, but never all at once. I disagree. Even with the mayhem and chaos of raising six kids and running a business, I've long felt like I have it all. I've often wondered if having it all is just simpler for me than it is for others. It must mean different things for different people.

My idea of having it all was to make labels until the wee hours and then get up and spend time with my babies from 6:00 a.m. onwards. My having it all included having six children. My having it all meant leaving a career I worked hard to get to so that I could better provide for my child with autism. Is it everyone's idea of having it all? Maybe not. In fact, a friend was once in line at an amusement park and overheard a couple of mothers talking about me. The gist of their conversation was that I must be run ragged, with all those kids and running a business and how awful it must be having my life, particularly since I also had a child with autism. My friend couldn't believe what she was hearing, especially since she knew I thought my life was perfect and I crafted it carefully to fulfill me and my family.

Did those moms in line think I had it all? Absolutely not, but it is not their business to define my happiness. So don't let anyone else define your happiness for you. The same goes for success, love, fun, and freedom. You cannot let anyone else draw those lines for you or chart those coordinates for you. This is your life. This is your business. This is your motherhood. You get to craft it to fulfill you and your family.

MOM ENTREPRENEURS: A LEGACY OF GUILT

I often joke that as the mother of six kiddos, I had to give up feelings of guilt about four kids ago. With such a busy life, I don't have the time or energy to focus on things that are unproductive. Feelings of guilt are useless to me. They don't make me a better mother or a better entrepreneur. Most of the time, when I'm feeling guilty, I find I either need to make a few adjustments to my life or I just need to forgive myself. Because lying awake at night and beating myself up is a ridiculous waste of valuable sleeping time.

Yet, mom guilt seems inevitable. Whether it's not spending enough time with your kids or worrying about focusing on your business, there are a few key areas where I think busy mom entrepreneurs end up falling into the guilt trap.

Mornings around our house are always hectic. I can vividly recall one day years ago when my then five-year-old woke up excited that the long-awaited kindergarten trip to the fire station had arrived. The best part was that I was going along as a classroom volunteer. She was such a mama's girl, so that was a pretty big deal in her little world.

This particular kid has always been a bit of a fashionista. By dumb luck, our kids ended up in a public school that had uniforms. As such, there was no real discussion about what kids were going to wear to school, which helped with our busy mornings. Still, my fashionista girl regularly expressed opinions about shoes, sweaters, and coats.

On the day of the school trip, the morning was madness. I had to get the kindergarten kid and the three biggies out the door. The baby was screaming for breakfast and the preschooler had to get dressed for nursery school. I was under pressure for time since I also had to get myself organized in order to be at school on time for the field trip. I handed my kindergarten kid her sweater with instructions to put it on and head out the door for the bus. She started fussing, complaining, and carrying on about not wanting *that* sweater. I snapped. Out of my mouth came something that stopped her in her tracks. I said, "If I get any fuss about this, I will *not* be going to the fire station." She looked startled and quickly put the sweater on.

I consider that statement to be a perfect example of lazy parenting. Did I really just threaten to take away something so special to her—spending time with me? Did I really just serve up a threat I would not have followed up on? Yep and yep.

Half an hour later, I was driving to the school with tears streaming down my face. When I arrived, my daughter's little face lit up. I gave her a hug and told her I was sorry about the sweater incident and that I would not have missed the school trip for anything. She laughed and said, "I know, Mama!"

I still get a lump in my throat when I think back on that, but I'm trying to remind myself that if my dear, sweet five-year-old could forgive me, maybe it's time to forgive myself.

Guilt and spending time with your kids

One of the main reasons women leave the traditional work force and launch a business is to go after the ever-elusive work/life balance. I certainly thought starting Mabel's Labels would allow me to spend more time with my children, and while it did, sometimes this time involved me working with my children around me.

Many years ago, one of my small children expressed significant dismay because I was on my laptop. I was overwhelmed with guilt. I mean, really: How could I expect my poor kid to entertain herself as I tried to grow a business? God forbid she had to play quietly with her siblings for a short period of time. Yes, at that time, I felt guilty, but

I've hardened up a bit since then. Kids *do* need to learn to entertain themselves. It's okay for them to *not* get the full attention of their parents all the time. It's even alright if they feel BORED once in a while. Yes, sometimes their needs have to wait because there are other people in the family who also have needs.

Clearly, no one wants to ignore their children or pay for the future therapy bills that may result, so finding the balance is essential. If you feel out of balance, make some changes. Be proactive. And let's not forget, mothers have NEVER paid attention to their children 100 percent of the time. Long before we were starting businesses from our basements or at our kitchen tables, children were being ignored by mothers who had to wash the laundry in the river. Mothers had households to run with none of the conveniences we have now. So before we start beating ourselves up for being the first generation of mothers who have things to do other than cater to their children 24/7, remember that mothers have never done that. Sure, we've all met that kid who gets endless attention from their parents. But from what I can tell, it rarely ever works out well for everyone involved.

Guilt and gadgets

As most working moms know, having our gadgets is an essential part of running our businesses. We are able to communicate, work on projects, market our businesses, and do a whole host of other things remotely because of technology. It's also something we struggle with because it can be really hard to turn off our gadgets and focus on our families. As business owners, we can find it hard to check out of work because we don't want to miss business opportunities. This inevitably leads to feelings of guilt.

Here's the way I see it. Yes, you do have to put your gadgets down and focus on your family. It's important to find those times. But I remind my children that it is because of technology that I am often able to work from home and be with them. The alternative would me being gone twelve hours a day working out of town in an office tower. They don't particularly like that alternative, so they are required to be patient and understanding of the work I do when I'm home.

If I'm attending a sporting event or watching them do an activity, I make sure they know what my gadget requirements are during that time. I may head into a hockey arena and say, "So you know, I have two emails to respond to and one phone call to take during your game." At all other times, they will have my full attention. If anyone has complaints, I remind them that without doing those few tasks while at the arena, I may not have been able to come and enjoy the game at all. As such, they know the lay of the land and I actually stick to it. They will not look up to the stands and see me with my head down typing the whole time. Communicating the plan is a win-win. They end up not feeling resentful of my gadget, and I end up feeling guilt free.

Guilt and social media

Social media is an inexpensive and fun way to connect with other business people and reach our market. Since social media takes a lot of the traditional "advertising" cost barriers away, it's no wonder entrepreneurs see the value and take advantage of using social media. We also use social media as a means to connect with other moms. We find our Mabelhood and communities online. It keeps us connected with other people who are facing the same struggles as moms and entrepreneurs. Sometimes we can get sucked into conversations and then feel guilty for the amount of time we have spent online. It's important to remember that having social connections has been an important piece for keeping mothers sane since the beginning of time. So our grandmothers may not have been chatting on Facebook, but they gathered for knitting circles, bridge clubs, book clubs, and various other social events. Connecting with other moms has long provided women with the support of other women folk. It has made us *better* and more informed mothers. Sharing opinions and information has helped us raise our families.

Guilt and me time

Admittedly, I don't get a lot of "me time." And I would advise against starting a business and having six kids if time alone is highly valued by you. Having said that, if you need to take that time, you better make sure you get it. It's extremely difficult to be productive at work and patient with your family if you aren't taking care of your own needs. Carve out time when you need it because it will benefit everyone you come in contact with. Don't fall into that false pride that comes with being "busy" all the time or pretending you don't need some down time. Know what you need and get it. Own it without embarrassment or feelings of shame.

But know that what you need won't necessarily be what others define as "me time." I learned that others meant that I should take time to sit in a coffee shop alone, go for a manicure occasionally, and spend time away from my business and my children. But I didn't want to do any of that. Here's the thing: I didn't find what many find relaxing to be actually relaxing. Not one bit.

I was once given a gift certificate for a massage because apparently someone thought I needed to relax. Relax, I did not. I spent an entire hour having my back rubbed while thinking about all the things I could have been doing during that time. That poor masseuse! There was nothing wrong with my thinking. My "me time" does not include having a massage, and that is okay! My idea of "me time" looked a lot more like being able to take a child to their hockey game with no toddlers to chase around, so that I could actually watch my little hockey player. To me, hearing the laughter and joy in my children's voices was fun! It was relaxing. To me, being able to have quiet time to work on a blog post, or create more labels, or record a podcast interview and actually connect with fellow entrepreneurs was relaxing! Building this business, though a hustle, was relaxing!

Much like not letting people project "having it all" ideals on me, I needed to reject traditional "me time" and allow myself to enjoy my life on my terms. But if you happen to enjoy traditional "me time," embrace it. Again, stay true to yourself and try to ditch the guilt and the feelings of having to adapt to how others think you should be, whether it's as a parent, a partner, or an entrepreneur.

Here are some tips that will help you conquer the guilt monster and help you stay in the green zone as an entrepreneur and a mom.

TIP: STAFF UP

I got a nanny when my fifth child was nine months old, which was about three kids too late. Don't be a fool like I was—give in and get the help you need! Don't feel like dragging a toddler and baby to the bus stop every morning in the dead of winter so you can get your bigger kids on the bus? Yeah, me neither. I enlisted an older student who goes to the same bus stop to do the morning pickup and afternoon drop-off for a cool $20 a week. "Bus buddies" are a good investment for busy mamas. Another good investment is a homework buddy. Homework is often a time of conflict for parents and kids because we are too darn emotionally attached. And things heat up when we get frustrated. I have a high school student come to the house, and my kids love having some time with their big kid friend. Homework is not something any of us dread anymore.

THE ULTIMATE MORNING ROUTINE TOOL

Tired of being a nag in the morning? Feel like a broken record barking out things like: "Don't forget your lunch!" and "Have you packed your homework?" Stop the insanity. Set up a simple system that will get them out the door while keeping your frustration levels down. Create a poster with visual cues that will help keep the kids organized and independent in the morning. A visual tool will help little ones manage their morning routines. If you do it on a magnetic board or a white board, kids can mark off each of their morning routine chores and head off for the day already feeling accomplished.

Moms who are entrepreneurs need to be highly productive. We have families to raise and successful businesses to run. Anything that acts as a barrier to your effectiveness has no place in your busy lives. Guilt is a predator. Don't allow it to sneak into your thoughts and prevent you from doing what needs to get done. And release the drill sergeant who dishes out guilt like it's their business—off with your head, Guilt!

#bizhack

Having it all could mean having an incredible month in sales and cash, or hiring the most aligned team member, or connecting with new biz besties.

#lifehack

"People don't buy what you do, they buy why you do it." –Simon Sinek

#momhack

Having it all can mean being present with your children in the moment and savoring their presence, their silliness, and their snuggles.

chapter four

Growth, Success, and the Love of Your People

Building a business is not for the faint of heart. Building a business with a group of four friends turned family turned business partners is even trickier, and not for the reasons you think. People often wonder, why four of us? Wouldn't there be misunderstanding? Miscommunication? What about growth? Who makes the decisions?

Yes, we thought of every single one of these questions. And if you are a small business owner who is in a business partnership with a friend or two, or perhaps considering it, my advice would be to stay open, keep the lines of communication crystal clear, and be kind—to yourself and to each other. From the very beginning, many people thought it was odd for a group of four to start a business. With multiple business owners, there is a lot of room for varied opinions and risk for conflict. While we have certainly had our fair share of feisty conversations around the boardroom table, we are able to make it work. Communication is key for us, and when we're doing it well, we function as a wonderful team. When we are not communicating well, we are not as effective. So communication is a top priority at Mabel's Labels. It's also a top priority within my family, and everywhere else I go. Although four co-founders may sound top heavy, in the early days it allowed us to divide up labor and responsibilities equally. We each brought something unique to the table and complemented one another's skills. Sharing duties resulted in quick growth.

However, as you continue to build a thriving business, it comes with its fair share of challenges and puzzles that you either figure out with a trusted loved one or mentor or expert (if you are a solopreneur), or in our case, with each other. Some of ours were:

Learning to let go

One of the biggest challenges for my partners and me was learning to let go. We were used to doing absolutely everything—from making the labels ourselves to licking the envelopes to writing press releases and filing taxes. The problem is, if you're doing every little task, you are not focusing on business growth. We had to shut down the little control freaks living within us and trust other people in order to work strategically to get our business to the next level. Trusting others and not micromanaging everyone and everything took a lot of practice. Because there will be instances when your people will make mistakes.

They will, they're human. But unless you trust in them, their specialty and capability, and allow them the opportunity to show you what they're capable of, you're going to be stuck spinning all the plates until one of them crashes, or you do. So learn to let go, Mama. Be the CEO you dreamed of being. Offload and let go of one task at a time. It takes time and practice, but I guarantee you, once you see it off your plate, the relief and spaciousness you feel will be palpable!

Filling the gaps

One morning at Mabel's Labels HQ, we looked around at our handful of staff and said, "Huh, we don't happen to know a thing about HR." As our business was growing, we learned to fill these gaps, and fast. Sometimes we would learn things ourselves, sometimes we would hire, and we learned that consultants are a great short-term solution. Hiring specialists and contractors who are good at what they do can change the trajectory of your life and business—this much, I am convinced of. Case in point, Mabel's Labels. Don't be afraid to fill the gaps in your business, in your household, and anywhere else. Free up your time so you can spend it on the things that truly bring you joy. Things that move your big vision forward.

Missing the good old days

I remember when decision-making meant sitting on the couch with a cup of tea and chatting with our few staffers. Things have changed a lot since then. It's natural to get sentimental for those days when things were so much simpler. Now we have meetings, committees, and procedures. This can be frustrating and seem cumbersome for the folks who have been around since the beginning because change can be tough to adapt to. We've learned that everyone copes better when we keep communication open and are transparent about plans and growth. We try to involve the staff and make them feel part of the excitement. Without our loyal and hard-working employees, there's not much to Mabel's Labels. Your people are everything, treat them well, nurture them, speak life into them, and enroll them in your vision. You'll be pleasantly inspired at just how much they also want the company and you to succeed.

Our successes are a measure of the quality of the product and exceptional service we have continued to put forth into the world. Awards and accolades are incredible, especially when you are congruent with your customer service, products, and people management. Some of our awards and recognition for our business and product excellence include a SavvyMom "Mom Entrepreneur of the Year"; "Best Product" from Baby Gizmo, iParenting and PTPA Media; an Outstanding

Business Achievement Award from the Hamilton Chamber of Commerce, and an RBC Canadian Woman Entrepreneur "Momentum Award."

As a result of our early and ever-evolving involvement in social media, we were named to *Inc.com*'s list of "20 Awesome Facebook Fan Pages" and *Hubspot*'s "The 15 Best Facebook Pages You've Ever Seen." We've been featured on *The View, Rachael Ray, Live with Regis and Kelly, The Early Show, Better TV, The Mom Show, Fox 5 San Diego, WGN's Midday, Parents, In Style, The Washington Post, People.com, Forbes.com*, and countless other media outlets and websites. Locally, we've appeared on *Canada AM, Breakfast Television, The Marilyn Denis Show, Metro Morning*, and of course, *CH Morning Live* (in Hamilton). Many celebrity moms have used Mabel's Labels, including Jennifer Garner, Rachel Weisz, Reese Witherspoon, Gwyneth Paltrow, and Victoria Beckham. Though proud of all this, achieving what we set out to do—putting out a quality product and providing customers with exceptional service—is our biggest mark of success.

#bizhack

Don't undersell yourself. A media coach may help you determine your value proposition and help create a bio and press. These can feel awkward to create ourselves because women often have difficulty sharing our qualities.

#lifehack

"Employees must love the company before customers ever will." –Simon Sinek

#momhack

Kids are not projects, so don't project your dreams onto them. They have their own dreams to chase.

chapter five

Know What You're Getting Into

Since we pioneered the original #mompreneur movement, as much as that title is outdated, entrepreneurialism is on the rise. Especially recently as the pandemic forced many to transition out of misaligned careers and jobs.

And I get it. The thrill of creating something, nurturing it, and watching it grow is extremely satisfying. It's like having a baby. And the life of an entrepreneur and the life of a parent have something else in common—people romanticize it. It is glamorized, and that is dangerous and misleading.

We see all those parents on Instagram with their beautiful babies wearing matching outfits while sitting in pumpkin patches, in fields of sunflowers, or on the beach. And we compare ourselves to them. We wish we were them. We don't like the grass on our side of the fence because we think it is greener on theirs. And it certainly looks like it from the highlight reel. We don't see them vomiting, dealing with mastitis, and cleaning up poop accidents. The same applies to entrepreneurs.

Many think the life of an entrepreneur is full of innovation, flexibility, notoriety, and lots and lots of profits, fame, media, Ted Talks, and accolades. And it might be, but it doesn't always start that way. Remember, we started in my sister's dingy basement with $100 to our name to invest in the business. It was not glamorous at all, yet it was to those who were on the outside looking in. What does it really look like? It looks like making labels in a basement through the night for years on end. It looks like never having a moment of "me time" because you are also doing a day job, raising a family, and tending to other life responsibilities. It looks tired and a little bit hungry. It also looks poor because when you're starting out, you worry about finances constantly and count every penny because every spare dollar gets invested back into your business with no real idea if you will ever succeed. Not very romantic now, is it? Not everyone has the grit to weather the storm that is entrepreneurship.

I also find that entrepreneurs are viewed as heroes. Certainly, it makes sense to honor their grit and risk-taking, but it's also worth noting that entrepreneurialism can come from a place of privilege. Often, those able to take the risk can do so because they have the financial means and support to take chances. I'm an example of that. I was able to leave the traditional workforce because our financial situation was stable. I could afford to take a chance. It's important to remember that—it's called privilege for a reason. We also hold serial entrepreneurs in high regard. But bear in mind, if they have one successful business that gets sold, they have the profits from that to take more chances. My point? Be careful when you romanticize entrepreneurs and the entrepreneurial life.

One of the things that attracted me to entrepreneurship was the notion of having flexibility, and it did provide me with that. I was juggling my son's program for autism, as well as raising his several siblings. I craved flexibility because to me it symbolized freedom. Something that I wouldn't have had while working as a lawyer. Nope. As a lawyer, my time would be billable in fifteen-minute increments, and I'd likely be glued to my office and phone. As an entrepreneur, I was responsible for how I spent my time, when I plugged into work. While I love working, I also love being available to my family during "business hours." So yes, I certainly have been that mom who can go to the pumpkin patch on the school trip (in fact, I'm sure I hold the record of school pumpkin patch visits after six kids). I loved being able to meet the other moms at the park in the morning with the kiddos, and it's great to be there to greet the kids when they get home from school. But, there's a catch. When people get excited about the notion of flexibility, I like to remind them that flexibility does not get your work done for you. If you are a fellow business owner who works from the comfort of your home, raise your hand if you've ever let flexibility get the best of you! I know I have!

Yes, attending those playdates and field trips, and volunteering at the school for events and activities is great— but you **will** be hunched over your laptop at midnight. The work still needs to get done, and you're the only one who is going to do it.

A question often asked of moms who start businesses is whether they've actually successfully found the ever-elusive *balance* in life. I juggle a lot of balls in the air and sometimes one gets dropped. I most appreciate when I am given the grace to take a moment to pick up that ball. I have to give myself that grace. Sometimes things will be out of balance. When it's back-to-school season and Mabel's Labels is nuts, I spend more time at the office. If I have a sick child or am dealing with an issue involving my family, I will spend more time with them. These are natural and can be expected; but day-to-day, I feel like I can achieve some sort of balance. If I feel like I'm getting it wrong or the dreaded "mom guilt" creeps in, simply shifting my focus is helpful. When I feel like I need to focus more on work or on home, I make changes that can allow that to happen. If I can't do that in the short term, I don't beat myself up for it. We cannot be our optimal selves at all times. I'm at peace with that. We are human beings, not robots.

Not only does an entrepreneur need to know what she is getting into when starting a business, but if you have a spouse or partner, you better make darn sure they are on board too. Have children? Communicate with them about what lifestyle changes can be expected with having a parent as an entrepreneur. Your spouse or partner needs to understand that date nights and holidays will probably be nonexistent, cuddling on the couch will be swapped out for working on your business, and they will likely carry the financial load for the family during a lot of uncertainty. If your family is not on board with your business venture and the accompanying lifestyle, things will get tricky. I've seen too many people see either their business or relationships fail because of unrealistic expectations. This is a game in managing expectations. And communicating openly—always!

I feel that with a little support, tons of open communication, and tight and clear boundaries and expectations, entrepreneurship doesn't have to be the emotional roller coaster that it can often be. Get your kids onboard with your mission and vision. Little eyes are always watching and learning. Get them involved in what you're working on, show them the behind-the-scenes of your business and what it means to you. You'll be surprised at just how cooperative they are and how inspirational they'll find it all.

BUSINESS PARTNERS—WHAT'S YOUR ARCHETYPE?

There is no question that most business advisers would say to steer clear from starting a business with too many partners. At Mabel's

Labels, we've made a habit of doing what feels right, so with that advice in hand, we went ahead and launched with four partners.

I think the partnership at Mabel's Labels worked well for so long because there were four very different people at the table, and I believe we had four different archetypes. When put together, it was clearly a recipe for success.

1) The Ideas Guy

People often wonder if the entrepreneurial spirit is a talent someone is born with or if it's something that can be learned. I think it's a bit of both. Just like a musician, someone can be born with musical talent, but another person can work and train and practice in order to master their craft. We certainly had one particularly entrepreneurial partner whose mind was racing constantly—it was one idea after another. This person brings an incredible amount of energy and innovation to an organization.

2) The Organizer

When the Ideas Guy would go running off on tangents with the "next big thing," the Organizer would rein in the group, see what the plan was, then find a pathway to execution. Sometimes perceived as the killjoy, this person was necessary for follow-through and to ensure procedure was followed. The Ideas Guy was the starter; the Organizer was the finisher.

3) The Level Head

When everyone is stressed, ideas are flying, hot-headed remarks are being made, and staff are freaking out, this is the one who reins in the entire team, reminds us to keep perspective, and works consistently to keep it all together. The Level Head is the glue of the organization and can communicate to everyone in a rational manner and in a way they can understand. They are also like the "mom" or "peacekeeper" of the organization because of their ability to manage all the different personalities. They are the trusted voice.

4) The Connector

This is the person who has contacts everywhere, gets the product out there, creates buzz, and makes the business exciting to those on the outside. The Connector pulls in networks and professionals and gets them interested in the business. They get the public to contribute their knowledge, skills, and circles to grow the business. This person is visible and credible. Without the Connector, a business may exist, but few will know about it.

It is quite common for entrepreneurs to be full of ideas. A common problem with having an idea is that it can sometimes become overwhelming. We fell into the habit of discussing an idea, deciding against it, and then revisiting it time and time again. That was a time-consuming exercise, and we'd often land at the same result. We had a wise business adviser warn us about spending too much time considering and reconsidering ideas. He used the analogy that ideas are like horses in the barn. Every once in a while you can march them past you to consider if they are still useful to the farm, then return them to the barn. But sometimes, it's time to put that horse out to pasture. Knowing when to put an idea to bed once and for all is a skill successful entrepreneurs need.

Almost twenty years into this gig, it has worked for us. There have been pitfalls along the way, but the advantages of our partnership far outweighed any disadvantages.

BENEFITS:

Divide and conquer. In the early days, we could divide up labor. No one person was responsible for every duty within the company. Each being able to contribute meant we could move along quickly and grow the business. Yes, this included being the cat-shooer.

Four brains are better than one. Between us, we had a varied academic and professional background. Everyone was able to bring their individual strengths to the table.

Feisty conversation. We had lots of fun and challenging banter around that boardroom table, but these conversations usually led to us making smart business decisions.

CHALLENGES:

Feisty conversation. Yes, I know it's in the Benefits section as well. We always had to be careful with our communication. Everyone receives information differently—it is important to be mindful of that, because careless communication can make for difficulty within the partner group.

We're family. We needed to make sure that whatever happens at work, we're still comfortable going to the cottage together and spending holidays and kids' birthdays together. I'm happy to report we successfully managed this while running the business, but I've seen a lot of other people not fare so well in this department. Is your business worth risking your relationships for?

Trust. Trust is an important ingredient for a successful partnership, but trust is also hard for entrepreneurs who have a tendency to want to do everything themselves and feel like they are the only ones capable of doing certain jobs. Trust is something that takes practice, and entrepreneurs have to keep on practicing—both with their partners and with their staff.

Think long and hard before you choose a business partner. I don't doubt for a moment that Mabel's Labels would not be where we are today if any one of the four of us were not involved.

#bizhack

Build a business that works for you. Set up a lifestyle and schedule that allows you to be both the business owner and the mama with clearly defined boundaries and communication.

#lifehack

"Life is like a taxi. The meter just keeps ticking whether you're getting somewhere or just standing still." –Lou Erickson

#momhack

Let your kids hear you speak positively about yourself. Share what you're proud of. They will do the same.

chapter six

Recession Entrepreneurs

The last two years have seen a rise in entrepreneurship amid an economic recession given the aftermath of the pandemic. Many of these businesses are owned by moms. These last two years opened up a window of opportunity that in essence was forced down upon us, since it's not something any of us could predict or control. Having the world come to a total standstill with everyone at home—working, learning, and doing all the things from home—meant that the *mother-load* was about to get heavier than ever. To the same effect, women, especially moms, in an attempt to bring in an income and stay sane either pivoted their brick-and-mortar businesses to an online store or started brand new e-commerce businesses. Many saw the pandemic as their opportunity to start the venture they've been dying to start or to go all in on their "side hustle." Wherever you fall on this spectrum and front, kudos to you! Whether you are in business or making moves in your corporate career during a recession, well done. This stuff is hard enough as it is, so keep going!

I always get asked, "Julie, is a recession a good time for mom entre-preneurs to launch a business?"

To that I'll often answer: "Is any time a good time to start a business? Because ready is never truly ready. It's a risk you take. It's a bet you make on yourself, your skills, your ideas, and your talent."

But, short answer: yes.

If you do your research, you will find various arguments for and against taking the plunge during these tough economic times.

Based on my experience, there are two major caveats to look out for when starting a business:

1) You are looking to launch a business and you recognize that it can take years (if ever) until you are able to take an income from the business. If your family is counting on you to take on the role of Sugar Mama, there will be a serious gap between expectation and reality.

2) The money-maker in your household is not at risk of losing a job because of the recession.

If you can check those two off your list, then there are many reasons why you might not put your business plans on the back burner just yet.

Often, what motivates a mom entrepreneur to start a business dif-fers from the motivations of a traditional entrepreneur. We embark into business ownership as a means of striking some balance and finding flexibility between our dueling lives of family and work. Many aim to supplement the family income enough to warrant a continued absence from the traditional workforce, while some have no intention of making an income at all. Running a small business can be a nice distraction from the daily grind of packing lunches and wiping noses.

If this is hitting home for you, Mama, I get it. These last two years haven't been easy; despite it all, you should be proud of yourself! For starting a venture, for exploring what this looks like for you and your family. And if you chose to intentionally take a step back, that's okay too. Nothing, and I mean nothing, is worth your mental and emotional well-being. The daily grind of motherhood can be a roller coaster, so it's okay if your business goals aren't your first priority right away. Do one thing a day that helps you move the needle forward.

If your goals are loftier than that and resemble those of Jessica Alba or Michele Romanow, it may be time to rethink the timing of your business launch.

Recession is not a time of rapid growth for business. Unless Oprah Winfrey herself knocks on your door (we're still waiting), the mom entrepreneur can use this time to manage growth at a pace that suits both her family and the economy. A recession promotes creative thinking and new ways of doing business. It brings out your curiosity and resourcefulness, and it also gives you the grit you need to succeed. Something I've observed over these last two years, and even during the 2008 recession, is this: There are businesses that will withstand the heat, the turbulence, and adapt themselves accordingly. They will go lean or pivot entirely. Whatever you choose, make sure that you and your family are able to navigate it as smoothly as possible, while also preparing for turbulence.

Unlike typical entrepreneurs, mom entrepreneurs are generally less risk averse. This works to their advantage during these tough economic times. Going to huge financial lending institutions and racking up a load of debt is unlikely. Imagine the mom entrepreneur sauntering into the bank for a loan, pitching her idea of making widgets at the kitchen table while dinner is in the oven and the baby is napping. I imagine the scene would resemble something I've seen on *Dragon's Den* or *Shark Tank.*

If a cash injection is required, the mom entrepreneur is more likely to hit up parents or in-laws, which is not high-risk financial behavior in a recession. If repayment has to be delayed for a couple of months, no one is going to come around to shake you down or break your kneecaps. Or repossess your home or car. This keeps your family grounded and anchored in some level of stability, while you are still able to pursue your creative ventures.

If you can get your business going in these times, then you have a pretty good chance of surviving anything. Any business born during times of necessity and crises is pretty much bulletproof, in that they can weather anything. Mom entrepreneurs are well rehearsed at watching the bottom line—it's what we do. If asked to trim down, it would be a difficult task to find where exactly to trim the fat. As a general practice, we resourceful moms don't waste time or money. If a marketing budget needs to be cut, we have the know-how to rely on our social networks and social media. You can catch the average mom entrepreneur on Facebook, Instagram, Twitter, TikTok, and on blogs. All that comes with a pretty good price tag attached.

Whenever we got overly cautious in the early days in the Mabel's Labels office, our feisty cousin who was our first marketing manager always gave us the same advice: "Go forth and be bold, and the mighty forces will come to your aid." I now pass those words to you. If you don't try something, you will never know. Opportunities are always all around you, within your Mabelhood, but you have to put yourself out there. You have to ask. You have to act. You have to be bold and take the first step. If the nudge in your heart is strong, and you cannot shake it off, you owe it to yourself to try something at least once. And go all in on it when doing so.

If there was one thing I learned in the last twenty years of entrepreneurship, it's this: Stay golden, stay humble. Do all things with greatness, and aim to be the best. Know your roots, anchor into your why, and keep going. When we started Mabel's Labels many years ago, we knew about tough times. We didn't have any airs and graces about us. Nor did we glamorize owning and founding a start-up. Our company was started in a grungy basement.

Our conditions were rough, but it wasn't too long before we were able to move into a more comfortable space. However, the lessons we learned in the basement have stuck with us and made us better business people for a whole host of reasons. I always tell my kids, "Remember who you are and where you come from. Don't lose sight of that."

Perhaps the most important lesson was that everyone starts in the "basement" or "ground level" as they call it in network marketing. It doesn't matter if you're starting a business, juggling a young family, starting a new career, or saving up for a car. You gotta start somewhere. You gotta roll up your sleeves and put in some elbow grease. The basement became our metaphor for that time in your life when you work day in and day out, wondering if anything will even come of your hard work.

I'm proud to say that there is so much that did come of our hard work and today, the business we started is very successful. But we still fondly remember our cat-shooing days (nights, actually), and this is what they've helped us remember: Don't forget about the people who were in the basement with you. This is everything!

There are people who you will meet on your journey in motherhood and in entrepreneurship who will help you navigate the mothership, and teach you the ropes, show you support, and cheer you on as you continue to launch your venture, and raise your baby, then another, and another. Keep those people close. Appreciate them. I remember in our early days, our friends, partners, mothers, and anyone else in our lives went out of their way to support us. This could also be your original staff members who shared those crazy working conditions with you. Many of ours have stayed with us all these years, supporting our business, taking pride in it, and always giving their all. As a result, we have tried to always let our staff know how important they are to us. We have a flexible workplace, we offer profit sharing, and provide a company culture that makes people feel loved so they'll stick around. Always give back to the people who looked out for you in your basement days. Don't forget about them! A kind word or gesture goes a long way. Gratitude, recognition, and appreciation are everything!

You don't have to have money to give

For years, we operated very lean. People often approached us for donations and contributions. We couldn't do it. We just didn't have the ability to give financially, but that doesn't mean we didn't give. We gave our energy and time. We helped fundraise and connect people to one another. Our amazing staff created a Community Relations Committee, and boy, did we give. Over the years, we have participated in Earth Day cleanups, adopted a park, fundraised for many organizations, volunteered at a children's hospital, sorted clothes at the Good Shepherd, performed many random acts of kindness, and the list goes on and on. If you don't have money, you can always give your time. There is always a way to give back to your community. Provide scholarships, barter time and energy, connect people to each other— you never know who might be desiring or needing that connection.

When the money starts coming in, share it

The first financial partnership we made years ago was with the Nanny Angel. This agency provides free nanny services to the families of mothers living with cancer. We provide both a financial donation as well as labels for all of the families that the organization works with as our way of helping out fellow moms during a stressful and difficult time in their lives. The Nanny Angel Network is a special and important organization to us for many reasons, but most importantly, because we're moms ourselves.

Gratitude, giving, and allowing resources to be distributed freely invites more abundance and positive energy, and who doesn't want that?! But more than anything, I know that if tables were turned and I needed a resource like that, it would mean the world to me if it were available. Give from the heart, it will always come back tenfold!

Most of all, we learned something key that we carry with us today. In the words of the Dalai Lama, "It's important to be kind whenever possible." And it is always possible. Giving is a part of who we are and our culture. It's easy to do no matter what stage of life you're in if you're creative and committed. Gratitude multiplies whatever you have and invites more of that into your life. There is always room to be loving, kind, and resourceful. We have a human and civic duty to look out for one another, why not start with being kind, generous, and grateful?

Many people think that one of the fast tracks to long-term success is the hustle and grind. Sure, that is part of it. But nothing takes you farther than having the humility to remember your roots and pay it forward, be a kind human being, cultivate and nurture genuine relationships, and have an open heart that seeks to create powerful impact. Your relationships are everything. How you treat someone says everything about you. There is always room to be kind. Always. Stay golden, friend!

Stay open to change and growth

It's no secret that entrepreneurship is on the rise. That said, the social media landscape continues to evolve. As business owners, it is up to us to stay open and curious to new trends, change, and implement what feels aligned for us. Though we may have virtual assistants, marketers, or a whole marketing team, it is up to us to be the face of our brand. To be the marketers, even when we have people helping us. Things change at the drop of a hat, so what is trending and working one month does not necessarily work six months later. Marketers have to be forward thinkers and thought leaders if they want to stay ahead of the game. The same goes for entrepreneurs. And if you are a mom, double whammy—you get to apply this lesson to motherhood too! Think about the way you convince your youngest child to eat their vegetables and clean up their toys vs. how you connect and relate to your oldest and try to get them to focus on school work and deadlines. Different, right? The same rules apply within marketing. You have to stay open and curious to growth and change.

If you are at the start of your career path or business journey, please make sure you love what you do. Why? Because the more you love it, the more you'll be able to show up and share your message online and in person with confidence. The more you love it, the more likely you are to be successful. Of course, we all have parts of our jobs that we don't like. But overall, when you enjoy and love the work you do—at a job or in your business—things flow smoothly. Stay open to evolution in your business, your team, and your vision. It's okay to not be where you started. It's more than okay.

And when in doubt, find mentors. This is extremely important. Not only seek them out, but actively ask them to mentor you and meet together regularly. This will contribute to your development and we will help you to be inspired. And stay the course of your vision, even if it evolves and pivots as the years go by. Ask yourself tough questions, and ask others tough questions. Don't be afraid or shy away from it. Good leaders and great entrepreneurs are willing to have the hard conversations. This is the best way to learn. If you don't know the answer, search it out. Don't try to fake your way through. Because faking it until you make it will only lead you so far. So embrace it, face it—don't fake it—until you make it, then face it some more.

Indulge your creativity. And encourage your staff to be innovative and entrepreneurial within their jobs. We do this at Mabel's Labels, and it has changed everything for us. To do this, managers have to give staff members room to breathe and experiment with their work. They also have to listen and reward innovative thinking. We set up brainstorming days and put groups together to inspire each other and build on each other's ideas.

Staying open to change and growth means knowing where your community is hanging out. Think of it like where all the kids go to party. You want to know their hot spots, so you can keep an eye on them. Of course, you're not stalking your audience, but it is helpful to follow the trends, stay informed, and get a feel for what your community wants next—a product, a course, or service. Our original audience was on

Facebook, as we all know the moms of our generation have Facebook. Our page has over 200,000 likes. As such, we are very active there. However, the new generation of moms love Instagram, so we show up there and now have 100,000 followers on that platform. TikTok is becoming more relevant every day, and who knows what tomorrow will bring. Meet your people where they are. I also blog for Mabel's Labels and have blogged on countless other sites as well to meet and connect with more potential customers. Having a vibrant social media presence is not only fun, it's good for business! And when you adapt and stay in the loop with change and embrace it, it embraces you too!

When I think of moms and entrepreneurs, I think of someone who is ready to stop, drop, and innovate! They are bursting with ideas and creativity. Rarely do they avoid change or fail to adapt. They know how to make something out of nothing. Now if that doesn't scream staying open to change and growth, I don't know what does. Change isn't always easy. It feels uncomfortable, sometimes icky and scary. But the flip side to change and evolution is sometimes incredible growth and success. So the next time you are hesitant to create an Instagram reel or try a new TikTok trend, I invite you to take the leap and just embrace it. You truly never know where these opportunities lead. Especially as more and more creatives and creators are able to now monetize their platforms on social media.

Your network is your net worth

When we started Mabel's Labels, there were very few online resources and no online communities. For the Mabel partners, at least we had each other. I really felt for solo entrepreneurs; if you couldn't physically get to events, you were on your own. It can be a very lonely journey if you don't connect with others in your position or those who have been there and can help coach and mentor you.

Your network is big—women are exceptional connectors. Tap into all of your networks. These include friends, mentors, other entrepreneurs, other parents, your staff team, etc. People are everything and business is indeed personal. If you find someone inspiring or want to learn from them, take them for coffee, send an email, pick their brain. There are so many online opportunities to connect as well. Don't forget about other parents. I'm the carpool queen and keep very close with my mama friends and neighbors. Moms who are at home with their kids are invaluable resources, and my experience is that they are very generous in helping out in a pinch for moms who might be stuck at work. Treat these friends like they are golden—because they are!

Get the right people on the bus

Your staff team is an invaluable network. Hire people who are more talented than you. Hire people who don't feed your ego, but fill your gaps. Hire smart people and give them power!

Curating a great staff team is time well spent. You want to fill your bus with a team that is committed, loyal, and understands the company core values. Hiring the wrong person is bad for business, morale, and costs in both time and money. We have learned the hard way how having the wrong people on the bus for too long can be toxic and impact your corporate culture. In our early days, we were reluctant to fire people because firing people is HARD. What is harder? Keeping them around and then having to recover from their negativity or incompetence. You will never sleep the night before you fire someone. Their work peers may not want to see their colleague fired, but they do want to see them gone. It will bring great relief to the rest of the team, and strangely, to the person you let go. They deserve to find a place of work that better suits them.

Create leaders and support other moms in your business

The best advice I can give is to leave your ego at the door and hire people who you will encourage to be leaders. Great leaders do not hire followers, they create more leaders. With Mabel's Labels being a women-founded business, the treatment of women employees (and all employees) has been important. How can workplaces be more inclusive of women? Organizations need to believe in and practice pay equity. Pay a living wage. It's important to ensure that a promotional pathway exists for women. At Mabel's Labels, we've had people working the night shift in production eventually become department leaders. A co-op university student became our first marketing manager. A woman who was contracted to help with a product launch now holds the highest position in the company. Investing in women's professional development and creating a culture where men get called out is essential. Hire men and encourage them to advocate for female colleagues.

We were four moms who started in the basement. We created this company at strange times and in strange places. We built business plans during nap time, did product research while at playgroup, and changed the world as we changed diapers. As such, we really understood that women could be hugely productive at nontraditional times and didn't necessarily need the confines of the traditional workforce. So, we've tried to be RESULTS driven. Meaning, if our team is meeting goals, that is what I care about.

Different horses for different courses

As your business changes, develops and grows, so might your staff network, and that's okay. The person you hired during the start-up phase might not be the person you need for the next level. As the course changes in your business, so must the players. When we were in the start-up phase, we needed worker bees in the production facility getting those labels out the door. We also needed generalists, because of our size. Our HR staff member had to be able to do high-level work, as well as rolling up their sleeves to write policy and help people fill out time cards. Our finance person was the same—a jack-of-all-trades.

As the business grew, we needed to make more specialized hires. Our most difficult transition as business owners was when we first hired managers. This can be tricky because entrepreneurs can often be control freaks and have a hard time handing over the reins. But the handing over has to happen. After all, if the CEO of a company is so busy during the week that they're not focused on the future of the company, then there will be no future. It's important that a CEO also doesn't micromanage their new hires, which is not good for retention. Sometimes stepping away and seeing that things can be done a different way works out for the best. We've certainly had to sit back as someone failed and learned. That is part of it all.

Customer service is the secret sauce

We are passionate about our customers and our customer service. There are many ways we show appreciation to our customers, be it through loyalty programs, rewarding brand ambassadors, and creating refer-a-friend programs. Some of our brand ambassadors have come through these channels, but most have come quite organically. They are customers who have fallen in love with our product and brand over the years from the great experiences they've had. Moms love talking about products they believe in. We have created brand ambassadors, in part, by creating an amazing product moms relate to.

Our customer service perspective is that we want our customers to be 100 percent satisfied, and if things go wrong, we exceed their expectations. For example, we'll replace labels that the customer themselves misspelled when ordering. This always comes back to us because those customers spread that wonderful Mabel experience far and wide.

An important part of getting customer service right is by giving your staff team the power and autonomy to use their own good judgment to make things right for customers. It's also great to give them the power to have fun in their roles. Some of the initiatives we've seen the team take is setting up a "Customer of the Day" program. They also have a "Wowing Wednesday" initiative, which is where the customer service reps recognize one special customer by doing something creative to really wow them. Our team also takes NPS (Net Promoter Score) surveys very seriously. They survey customers every month and include a box for free-form comments along with the rating. Each month, the reps work through the comments and take the time to address all of the complaints. Most customers are shocked and grateful that someone is a) reading their feedback and b) solving the problem. They aren't expecting to hear back from a survey. Promotions and gamification are also very engaging. Monthly promos may not always result in increased revenue, but it gives something for us to engage our customers with. Our customers love our weekly contests on social media and enjoy tuning into the content we provide.

Be results focused with your team

My experience has always been that when you treat people like grownups, they act like grownups. In our culture, although we love gathering and working together at the Mabel's Labels headquarters, we have a culture of being results focused. When you empower your people to lead themselves, and show them you trust them immensely and celebrate their unique gifts, you'll be surprised at just how much they show up for you fully!

Lessons learned in the business trenches

They say if you want to radically change your life and go through massive growth, start a business. And that saying has been true in my life. Building this business with six children has been rewarding and fulfilling in every way. In every aspect of your business, however, you want to ensure you are working with the right people, whether they are your business partners, suppliers, or other companies that you collaborate with.

If you are considering starting a business with a partner, there are many things to be aligned:

- Do a skills inventory. Does your partner fill gaps for you?
- Do your personalities work together?
- How does the other person communicate? What is their communication style?
- Are your goals aligned? What do you want from the business now and in the years ahead?
- Consider personal lives and priorities. If one partner prioritizes personal life and the other prioritizes professional life, you might want to discuss these differences.
- What are your core values?

Remember that your personal brand and professional brand are connected

Think you don't have a personal brand? Think again. Personal brands exist and not just for the Martha Stewarts, Oprah Winfreys, and Kim Kardashians of the world. I remember the moment I discovered how important my personal brand was to Mabel's Labels. Someone expressed how much they liked my brand, and I misunderstood and assumed they meant the brand of Mabel's Labels. But I did have one, just like everyone does, and it is particularly helpful and useful for entrepreneurs. We often think only famous people or celebrities are brands. This is simply not the case. It is worth considering how your personal brand can leverage your business. Your personal brand is very connected to how the world sees you. Your personal brand is based on the impression you make on someone, the way you present yourself to the world. Every action you take has an effect on your personal brand—whether it be an interaction, a social media post, or a speaking engagement. People who consider their brand when they are in the public space are usually the ones who end up with respect and opportunities.

In addition to being a business owner, my brand includes being a mom to a big family, being an autism mom, a parenting blogger, and a media parenting contributor. And I've been able to use my personal brand to elevate the Mabel brand.

In creating or defining your personal brand, there are a few areas to consider and focus on:

Be authentic

No matter how much people try, they can't avoid projecting who they really are. They may fool themselves into thinking people see them differently, but ultimately, the truth comes to the surface. The brand you design must be true to who you are. It should be consistent with your core values, your skills, and your history. Being self-aware helps a lot here.

If you think you might have blind spots, consider this simple exercise:

- Write down a list of adjectives that describe you, then ask the few people who know you best to do the same. Compare the lists for common descriptors.

A strong personal brand can protect you from being copied or imitated. Certainly, I tell every entrepreneur that their idea WILL get replicated. Another company will be a fast follower and try to profit from your innovation. But no one can imitate your story. For Mabel's Labels, it was four moms starting a label empire in a creepy basement while their babies napped. What is your unique story that separates you from your competitors? More and more, customers want to feel a personal connection with an individual CEO. Your personal brand will create that connection and make you stand out among competitors.

I have even had a situation where someone has tried to imitate my voice. They adopted my writing style and even used words and phrases that are typical of me. Customers and friends were outraged. I was not very bothered, because at the end of the day, that writer would find her own voice. She couldn't use mine forever. Eventually your authentic voice comes out, and when you don't use it, people notice. As such, she finally found her own voice. There is only one me and no one can take that away. Those others who try to be anyone else will fail and damage their brand in the meantime. So don't worry about the fakes. And believe me, your audiences, customers, and especially the mamas can sniff out a fake. So be you!

Know your audience

If you don't know who you're selling to, you're done. The more information you have, the better chance you have of selling. We figured out fairly early on that *moms* are our audience, and they also are the ones making purchasing decisions for their families. But we always strive to do more than just sell to them. Behind every decision we make, we ask ourselves, "Are we making these moms' lives easier?"

We consider this with our social posts, blogs, label application tutorials, and every product we launch. We know moms want community, so we created that as well. Our market wants to feel connected to their brands, which is where my personal brand comes in. They don't want to buy from a nameless, faceless corporation. They want to buy from brands they trust, and visibility and connection to a personal brand does that. I blog, not about labels, but about being a busy mom who is also trying to get through the day without losing my cool with bickering tweens. Moms place a lot of value in trust. So what do they trust? It's not traditional advertising, which is why community and influence are so important to today's mom. Knowing your audience and how they receive their content is key.

Building a strong community within our Mabel brand is what our audience wants. Moms support brands they can relate to. If they trust you, they're listening. If they're loyal, they're buying.

Product "YOU"

There are certain people who truly live the brand of their company. Bring your face to the brand. People are overrun with products and businesses. They are marketed to constantly.

Remember, your story is what sets you apart from your competitors, and everyone has a story. Many businesses are set around lifestyle, so you can leverage the credibility of a personal brand, which establishes you as an expert. I've done that very thing. I do morning shows about prepping kids for camp, getting them out the door on the first day of school, and about organization for all sorts of things. If anyone is writing an article on women and entrepreneurship, I'm front of mind. By setting yourself apart, you get many opportunities. And you can set yourself apart with your story, sharing it, and being true to your brand. And this is good for business. I have a lot of evidence that tells me that being an "expert" sells Mabel's Labels.

Your brand voice

I bring my face and my voice to the Mabel's Labels brand. You don't have to have a big brand and name, but you are your business. I believe what sets us apart from big corporate companies is that I let people in. I share photos of myself and tell my stories. It is the Mabel's Labels way—we let people in, and they love a big warm community.

One effective way to build trust is to get out there! People equate credibility with visibility; the more they see you (in a consistent manner and tone), the more they perceive you as better and see you as competent. Being visible is so important, and it provides you the opportunity to connect in a consistent and reliable way.

What happens when your brand changes? I'm a good example of that; I went from having six babies to six teens (actually, my two oldest are now in their twenties!). My customer is a different demographic than me now. It's okay to do a rebrand. I don't talk about diapers anymore, but we've got people on our marketing team who are the demographic of our audience and customers. You will still be yourself and have your same core values, but if you are changing up your subject matter or presentation, your audience will notice. Again, be transparent and talk about the rebrand. If you've created a strong personal brand, your audience will follow.

Can your professional and personal brands be divided?

My short answer is no. I can write in my social media bios "views are my own," but I can assure you that if I share an unpopular view, that will impact my business. There are countless examples of businesses that have failed or been negatively affected by the thoughtless words of their CEO or founder. Even if employees represent themselves poorly in public, it impacts business. This is why many companies are training their staff in social media and PR, and quickly firing them when they misstep. Business owners work very hard to create a strong brand and don't want it being tainted by a careless staff member. Your comments will be linked to your company.

Can brands protect themselves?

Don't let different people be your voice to avoid inconsistency. Having one consistent voice is helpful. If you are going to have anyone do social media for you or your brand, be sure to vet their content for a very long time to ensure they understand your voice and your style of messaging. Having team members on social media can be a great way to spread the word about your company—they are often your best brand ambassadors. It's helpful to ensure that they go through a company certification program outlining social media expectations. If they don't want to mention working for your company, then no need to certify. At Mabel's Labels, any team member who talks about the company has gone through our little certification program. It's a way of protecting our brand. Another tip is to make sure you never delete negative comments from your social media pages. Use them as an opportunity to engage your audience and let them witness you remedying the problem. Clearly, if a comment is inappropriate and not related to your business or it is abusive, delete and report.

Tools for branding yourself

Determine your branding channels. These are the avenues, the manner in which you'll disseminate your brand message. This could include referrals, public seminars, social media, direct mail, advertising, blogging, publishing, online radio, editorials, video blogging, networking, television, article writing, PR, conferences, etc. Be sure your overall message is consistent throughout all of your branding channels. Use effective visual branding ensuring your website, social media channels, business cards, etc., are consistent too.

Get comfortable being uncomfortable

The thing with starting a business is that as soon as you get comfortable with where you are at, things change. Growth creates constant change. One minute you're working in a basement, next you're looking for a commercial space to run your production facility out of. One minute you're asking your mom to help pack up labels, next you have a team of staff and have to figure out Human Resources and write job descriptions. There is constant change, and it helps to have an appetite for risk. We have a sign on the wall at Mabel's Labels that says, "If you are not living on the edge, you are taking up too much space."

We've always tried to set goals and to create stretch goals as well. Staying innovative and thinking outside the box is a necessity. Always challenging yourself is important. As the saying goes, "If you're the smartest person in the room, find a new room."

I know it can be uncomfortable applying for business awards, but

I highly suggest it for three reasons. The first is that the application process often forces you to dust off and revisit that old business plan and define your goals. It makes you take stock of your finances and if you are on track. That is information you should always keep an eye on, but busy entrepreneurs get distracted so applying for awards is a great way to keep yourself in check. Awards also provide some great public relations opportunities. If you happen to win, there is usually a well-run campaign in the media that will highlight you and your business. Finally, winning an award can position you as an "expert" in your field, which provides more opportunities. I know applying for awards can be difficult because women are generally not great at self-promotion, so you can always enlist help with the process.

The lessons we learn in the trenches of business are lessons we can apply into other areas of our life too. I strongly believe that how you do one thing is how you do everything, and it shows. What happens in your personal life will inevitably flow into your career or business. You are human, and you will make mistakes—tons of them. Give yourself enormous amounts of grace. Remember the lessons from each experience and keep on keeping on. Elevate yourself and others, pay it forward, and celebrate yourself and others. Celebrate your growth, how far you've come, all the milestones, all the small wins! Set the bar high for yourself and others—in work, life, and in motherhood. Stay attuned to your core values, your truth.

#bizhack

Be visible. Want to get media? Make sure you have a great headshot, a nice press page, and a reel, if you can. Get pitching. If you want to be invited back for an appearance or segment, make sure you look camera ready AND make the producer's job as easy as possible. Send a clear segment outline, even suggesting host questions.

#lifehack

"Match my hustle!" Katie, my hairdresser, to any man who wants to date her.

#momhack

Balance is a game of managing expectations. Be transparent with your kids about your work for the day so they know what to expect. Then stick to it!

chapter seven

Own the Mothership

Seriously, I have that Beyoncé song playing in my head on a loop. Because, damnit, we do run the world—we're birth leaders, change makers, dream chasers, and so much more. We birth businesses and babies, and sometimes even ourselves. With the birth of each child, the mother is often reborn. And six children later, I can definitely tell you that I run my world as best as I can. #likeamother. I once had the pleasure of having the National Parenting Columnist for CBC, Karen Horseman, come to my house for an interview on the topic of "striking the life/work balance." She asked if we could provide some background noise that would be appropriate for the segment. I let her know that noise was our specialty and we could serve it up anyway she liked it. We could do background noise, headache creating noise, noise that makes the walls shake, playing in the pool noise, noise in the form of shrills, screams, cries, and laughter. We could even make the kind of noise that gets neighbors calling the city council. Wouldn't be the first time.

When we first realized that the Mabel co-founders were the emerging "poster child" of the mom entrepreneur scene, we were thrown a bit off guard. We thought of ourselves as entrepreneurs and initially bucked the label. It was when we realized that Mabel's Labels exists and everything we do is based on our mamahood that we came to terms with the title. At the time, the term went straight to the heart.

Yes, as moms, we often trade in luxuries like sleep, proper meals, and reality TV viewership in order to have some flexibility, but it was a choice we made very deliberately. We often reflected on the following quote after we won the Mom Entrepreneur Award, as it sums up our experience well:

"A Mom Entrepreneur starts a business to be able to make choices. We choose to live as dynamic business owners, enthusiastic mothers, and inspired women."

We thought it sounded better than our original quote of: "In our hormonally imbalanced and irrational states, we choose to live as overworked and underpaid business owners, exhausted mothers, and neurotic, and somewhat manic women."

Mama, perhaps you are in a season of life where motherhood feels heavy, exhausting, and you are also building your dreams. Maybe it feels like you have to choose. Or maybe everything is flowing in its natural rhythm. Perhaps there are labels that you may not want to wear right now. Perhaps it's the identity of motherhood and the motherload that keeps you stuck. Maybe you're wondering: *Who am I now? After the kids?* I invite you to shift that perspective. What is being a mother teaching you? Where is it guiding you? How is it propelling you forward toward your vision for your family and dreams? What is something you'd trade off in a heartbeat to do what you love AND be home with your kiddos? Or how can you embrace the dualities of motherhood, womanhood, and being ambitious and driven at the same time? I encourage you and invite you to build a lifestyle and vision that aligns with your family's needs, and most of all, your needs. And though this will have its challenges, it is so worth it!

BALANCE IS WHAT YOU MAKE IT

People often wonder how I strike a balance between being a business owner and a busy mom. You don't always. But you can create a blueprint that helps you come close enough, and that's good enough for me.

When you're an entrepreneur, having a holiday completely disconnected from work is almost impossible. My situation is even a bit trickier because I'm the company spokesperson. I get calls or emails from media folks at all times of the day and quite frankly, I don't want to miss them. Indeed, it's my job NOT to miss them. If someone reaches out at 8:00 p.m. for a quote to go to press in the morning, I'm giving them a quote and tucking the kids into bed at the same time.

So how do I disconnect with work so that I can connect with my family? I'll admit, I don't have it mastered. I don't always get it right, but I keep on trying. Here are three things I strive to commit to:

Don't have the laptop open during family movie night

We've all tried this one. And I know as hard as you try, it backfires. We think we can trick our kids into believing we're watching a movie with them while we get a bit of work done. The thing is, sooner or later someone says, "Hey, Mom, I don't get what just happened" and you're caught. We think it's acceptable to do because we're not actually "doing" anything with them, just watching TV. For anyone who questions whether TV is social, just hop on Twitter when there's a new *This is Us* episode and watch the banter. TV is social and there are plenty of opportunities to engage around the boob tube. Besides, actually being with your kids instead of faking it is way more fun. So for a change, ditch the phone and the laptop. Your heart and your kids will thank you for it.

Watch them play sports, or sing, or dance

Of course there are occasions where you have to send an email or answer your phone while attending one of your child's activities. I try to warn my kids when I am expecting a call and let them know that they may look up once in a while to see me distracted by a work call. They understand that. But imagine your child scoring their first goal and excitedly looking up to you for a cheer only to find you staring down at your gadget. Yes, that was the sound of your child's heart breaking in disappointment. That email doesn't seem so important now, does it? Whenever possible, try and be present in the moment. And again, give yourself grace for the moments you are having an all too human moment and are juggling the motherload and all that comes with it.

Wrap up that call before you walk through that door

We all know it's a big "no-no" to walk in the house after a day at work while on a phone call. Nothing says "I love you" like shushing and motioning kids away when they are greeting you enthusiastically. Many parents sit in the driveway to finish off that call. Personally, I don't even pull into our court. I never know who will be playing outside or waiting at the window watching for my car to pull up. I finish calls on side streets so that my enthusiasm will match theirs when we are reunited after a work day. I believe our energy is priceless, and sure, we might feel incredibly exhausted juggling all the balls, but our presence, our whole self, and the energy with which we show up to things matters. It matters to your kids, your partner, your clients, and most of all to you.

Sometimes I get it right and sometimes I don't. And sometimes readjusting takes place.

GUILT SCHMILT

It's pretty fair to say motherhood and guilt go hand-in-hand. If you haven't felt the elusive mom guilt, do you even mom? I have six kids and went to Catholic school—a combination of factors that should provide more than enough guilt to keep me awake at night. The thing is, I'm already sleep-deprived and not about to hand any precious shut-eye over to guilt. And I have no room in my busy daytime life for guilt either. Quite simply, I don't have the energy to entertain such nonsense.

I haven't always been this comfortable about living without guilt. When I was a first-time mama, I gained membership into a club no parent wants to be a part of—my son was diagnosed with autism. I settled quickly into my new role as his advocate. I made sure he received the best possible therapy, and he flourished. Nothing was going to get in the way of his progress. But there was one question that continued to haunt me and stood in the way of my own progress through his diagnosis: *WHY did he have autism?* I would repeat the same questions over and over in my head: *Was it something I did while pregnant? Did I eat something with mercury in it? Did I wait too long before agreeing to have the emergency C-section?*

You see the pattern, right? Every question involved self-blame. Why did I feel compelled to pin the autism on myself?

It finally occurred to me that knowing what caused his autism was not going to make it go away. Besides, his diagnosis didn't change the way I loved or felt about him. Why did the *why* matter? That realization was my defining moment—I was shutting the door on blame and guilt. Good riddance. Adios! Bye forever!

As moms, we can find plenty of reasons to feel guilty over just about every choice we make: whether you did or didn't breastfeed, co-sleep, use cloth diapers, baby wear, vaccinate, make organic baby food, work outside the home . . . you get the gist. We can find a way to feel guilty about most things. We're not all that selective. There are, however, two particular areas where we are most vulnerable:

1) THE "WORK/LIFE/KID/FAMILY/PROFESSIONAL GROWTH/ BALANCE" JUGGLING ACT.

Kids demand a lot of attention and as mamas, we generally want to give it to them. But the reality is that sometimes we have to get other work done, whether it's dealing with a client or getting dinner on. Their disappointed little faces when we can't do what they want when they want it can sometimes leave us feeling like substandard parents. But I assure you, you are not. Trust me. You are doing everything you possibly can, your best in each moment, so ditch the guilt wagon.

I once had a three-year-old tell me she gets a stomach ache when she sees me working on my computer. Ouch—that hurt. But sorry about your luck, kid, sometimes I have to send an email from my phone while at home with you. Other times, I need to shut the door on my home office to take a phone call even though you want me to read a book at that very moment. I am sorry if you think it's unfair, but I'm not sure the alternative would suit you much better. Not having my own business would mean me spending long days in a law office, while you and your siblings are in full-time daycare. There would be no flexibility for afternoon playdates, no morning walks to the park, and definitely no picnic lunch dates. How does your stomach feel now, kid? Striking that work/life balance is a constant work in progress for all mothers. We don't need to add a dash of guilt to the mix of our already ridiculous balancing act.

2) THE "WOW, DID I EVER MAKE A BAD MEDICAL JUDGMENT CALL" MAMA MOMENT.

Okay, so I am going to confide in you that one time I let one of my kids walk around on a broken foot for three weeks before taking him for an X-ray. Did I feel bad about it? Well, it wasn't my proudest moment. Should I have gone to the hospital earlier? Sure. But he wasn't complaining, and we all know how hard it is to decide whether an injury warrants a trip to the emergency room. Haven't we all taken a kid to the hospital who we thought had a broken limb, only to turn around and see the injured kiddo doing cartwheels in the waiting room? I have as much confidence in my decision to go to the hospital as I do choosing a horse at the racetrack. And I invite you to trust your instincts, no matter what. And give yourself enormous amounts of grace. It's all a crapshoot—sometimes we call it right, sometimes we don't. On this occasion, I lost.

Another time, I made an appointment to take our then six-month-old to see the doctor. His cold had been dragging on, and I thought we should get it checked out before he spent the night with my friend, while we attended a family wedding. The doctor took one look at my babe and announced he was in respiratory distress and called the pediatrician to meet us at the hospital. I may not be getting a "Mother of the Year" award for that medical mishap, but beating myself up over missing the signs would have been a colossal waste of time. Guilt doesn't do anything but keep you stuck in the past when in fact you could be focusing on a solution for the present and the future.

And that is exactly the point. Guilt steals time from people who have no time to waste. I'm already physically and emotionally exhausted from everything I do. There is no room in my already overcrowded brain for the "what ifs." It's full and I've put up the CLOSED sign!

I like to compare the futility of feeling guilty to the futility of complaining. Both achieve nothing. Believe me, I've tried saying, "I'm tired" to see if it would miraculously result in more sleep. It didn't, so I haven't bothered saying it again. Let's face it, we're all tired. Mamas have little humans who get up in the night to do things like drink milk, cut teeth, be sick, go pee. It's exactly what we signed up for when we had kids. Complaining about it is just boring.

Same goes for guilt. Does guilt make your life more complete? Does it contribute to the happiness of your family and friends? Is it fundamentally proactive to lie in bed at night tossing and turning, reflecting on what a bad mother you are?

Sure, we all want the odd "do-over." Instead, take the lessons you learn on your parenting journey and apply them in the future. And if your kids still screw up, remind yourself that it's probably because of an inherited personality flaw, probably compliments of their father.

Let go of the guilt. There will be no trips to the house of mirrors to point blame at this overworked mama. I suggest you make the same pledge.

LOWER YOUR STANDARDS

Yes, that's right. Sometimes mine are so low I'm surprised I don't trip over them. There is a theory called gold plating in business and project management. It is the phenomenon of working on a project past the point of diminishing returns. There are a lot of risks associated with gold plating in business, including working outside of the project scope and going over budget. I've seen my kids do the same thing on occasion: spend ten hours working on a school project that will get them at 85 percent. They would need to spend an additional ten hours to get to a 90 percent. I'd argue that it's not worth it, particularly in the case of busy working moms who have a lot on their plates. Sometimes things are "good enough." This can be a very difficult outlook for people who struggle with perfectionism. Fortunately, I've managed to avoid that personality trait. A bullet dodged, as the case may be.

I have a friend who is very organized and does certain housework on certain days of the week. She washes all the sheets once a week. Yes, every week—even when there's no urine, vomit, or phlegm on them! Around my place, sheets get washed when there is a reason to. Again, this is about priorities. For me, having a perfectly clean house and wonderful home-cooked three-course meal every night is not one. When people walk in my house, they will likely notice that it is a bit messy. What's the worst that can happen? Perhaps they will tell people that my house is messy, and they'd be right. I genuinely don't care about those kinds of reports. When people come to my house, they generally feel welcomed and at home. In fact, if they arrive early to a party, guests will likely be assigned a chore. No one at my funeral will talk about how my crystal sparkled or my china tea cups matched, and I'm okay with that.

There are times when it is particularly important to lower your standards. The times I am most forgiving of myself is when I have had a new baby arrive or when it is August and Mabel's Labels is going crazy with back-to-school orders. I am not going to be *Mom of the Year* during these times. When I have a newborn, I'm okay with letting the kids have hot dogs for dinner two nights in a row. If they are watching a little too much TV, I'm not beating myself up. When I'm not my optimal self, I give myself the reminder that this will be for only a certain amount of time. The kids won't get scurvy from lack of vegetables nor will they get square eyes from watching a little extra TV.

GET HELP

I remember the cycle of thinking when I left the traditional workforce to start Mabel's Labels and be with my children. I refused to get help for so long because it felt counterintuitive to get help with the very children I wanted to be home with. Alas, this thinking was flawed, but it was not until my fifth child was a year old that I caved and got a full-time nanny. It was a game changer. Suddenly I could be engaged with my kids AND more productive in my work. Knowing when to get help is a skill, and I'm annoyed it took me so long to recognize the need. I suggest that every family needs to at least get a cleaner to come to the house every couple of weeks. That way the deep clean is done and you can easily maintain. I know, I know . . . it can be expensive. To that, I say feed the children more instant noodles! This is money well spent and should be a priority. It is certainly a lot cheaper than marriage therapy, and hiring a cleaner may save you from needing one!

THE PITFALLS OF MOTHERHOOD (AND LESSONS FOR BUSINESS)

Yes, there are pitfalls. As much as I am all pro the roller-coaster bonanza that is motherhood, much like the highs, I am no stranger to the lows. One event occurred that made me realize I didn't recognize who I had become, nor did I like who I was becoming. This realization dawned on me after my first child was born. When I had Mack, I was blown away by how much I loved him, and I really wanted everything to be just perfect. I also fancied myself as the baby expert and got a little bit bossy. My moment of clarity came while watching Daddy-o bathe our new baby. From where I was sitting, the bath water was too cold, the soap was all wrong, the washcloth was forgotten, and the non-fluffy towel was chosen. And I seemed unable to keep myself from commenting on each and every one of these ridiculous observations. It was like my mouth had a mind of its own. No one enjoyed bath time that night and the feeling it left stayed with me for a long time.

Since that time, I have become skilled at noticing the little ruts we can find ourselves in—the patterns and attitudes that transform good moms into people we don't recognize. I've sorted these morphed-mamas into categories I like to call: the Critic, the Nag, the Scorekeeper, and the Complainer. These extremes sometimes pop up in the business world. Whether you're dealing with a partner (or spouse) at home or a partner (coworker) at work, it's important to make sure you stop yourself from morphing into one of these.

THE CRITIC:

This is the bath time experience I just described. The Critic believes that her way is the best way and a pattern emerges:

- Dad attempts to interact and care for baby.
- Mom disapproves and helps by providing suggestions (a.k.a. criticism).
- Dad loses confidence and is reluctant to care for baby.
- Mom gets frustrated and resents dad for not pulling his weight.

Mama has now created her own monster, a self-fulfilled prophecy, of sorts. Dad has been made to feel useless, so that is exactly what he becomes. I saw myself fall into that trap, so I made the decision to only comment when a child's health or safety was involved. So, if our kid had a dirty face, I said nothing. Dressed funny and not matching? No comment from me. I once came home and found every child was dressed in the outfit of a sibling. No kid was wearing anything that fit them properly. What did I say on that occasion? Zilch. Absolutely nothing. These were not health or safety concerns. Besides, what did it even matter? It was important that I reminded myself often when the kids were small that my way wasn't perfect, it was just my way, not the right way, and it's not better than Daddy-o's.

Before the Critic speaks, she needs to ask herself, "Does it really matter?"

THE NAG:

What differentiates the Nag from the Critic is her tone of voice. We know she can be polite and respectful because we hear her talk to her friends and her mother. However, when the question or favor is directed at her husband, the tone completely changes and all "pleases" and "thank-yous" are completely abandoned. When mamas are exhausted by a new baby or energetic children, it's easy to fall into the habit of barking orders at hubby. At the end of the day, it doesn't make either parent feel good. If this defines your style, it's time to reshape how you communicate before it backfires and the kids start using the Nag tone with you!

THE SCOREKEEPER:

This is the mama who thinks diapers should be changed according to a schedule of "whose turn it is." If hubby is going out with friends on Friday night, you better believe Mama's going to spend all day Saturday at the gym or shopping. After all, it's only fair! This is a pattern

I desperately try to avoid. I strongly believe children can interpret this scorekeeping as parents getting "stuck" spending time with their children. Kids should feel that both parents want to be with them all the time—even during those times we might not.

THE COMPLAINER:

I don't think there's anything wrong with having a good rant with your girlfriends; they can make for good sounding boards. But the Complainer takes it to a higher level. She can recognize herself by asking if the phrase "I'm tired!" finds its way into every conversation she has. A sub-category is **the Competitive Complainer**. This describes the mom who has to one-up anyone who complains in her presence. If husband had a tough day at work, she had a tougher day at home. The reality is, being tired is what we signed up for as parents, and it is exclusive to no one. If this sounds like you, remember that complaining is not proactive. If there is a problem, do something about it. Magical naps don't appear just because you're tired.

Motherhood is hard work, very hard work. It's no surprise that at various times during this journey we find ourselves developing some of the symptoms that put us into one of these morphed-mama categories. I've learned that catching myself as the Critic, the Nag, the Scorekeeper, or the Complainer makes me unhappy with my behavior and certainly doesn't make any valuable contribution to my family.

We all find ourselves falling into these ruts from time to time, but with some quick recognition of the signs, there's plenty of time to climb out!

DON'T CREATE A MONSTER

If we want to be productive and have a healthy homelife, we don't want to turn our children into monsters. When I had six small children, it was often worth investing the time in getting them to learn skills to make them independent. I simply did not have the time to go around and zip up every coat. Getting out the door was a gong show at the best of times. Taking a few extra minutes to create independence in the kids paid off large. I know sometimes when we are in a rush, it's easier just to do things for the kids; this is particularly true when you only have one or two. With kids, short-term easy turns into long-term hard very quickly. Invest in them when they are small so that they will be independent and helpful bigger kids.

I know one mom who is both a neat freak and a control freak. When her two children were small, they were barely allowed in the kitchen. She would always pour their milk for them to avoid a mess. Guess how that ended up for her? She has two teenagers who lie on the couch and bark orders at her to fetch them glasses of milk. Moral of the story: let them pour their own milk and if they spill it, have them clean it up as well. No one likes taking orders from teens. Don't create those monsters.

Homelife and worklife have some interesting parallels. Getting help at home and at work is essential. At Mabel's Labels, we have contracted professionals and hired coaches to help us do better and assist in growing the business. There is no shame in getting help, in fact, you are doing your business a disservice by not getting new and bright professionals at your table.

We see employers create monsters all the time. Whether by poor leadership, micromanaging employees, not participating in creating a good work culture, or allowing toxic employees to stay on. These actions will make your team less functional.

Feeling judged brings out your inner monster

Modern momming is a whole new jungle. Everywhere you turn, you get stares, opinions, and possibly even trolled (especially if you're a part of all the online groups and share an opinion contrary to the majority). It definitely has its perils—we're not only being judged by those older than us, we're trying to keep up with each other while worrying about what the next generation is thinking. I remember once taking my three youngest kids for lunch at the food court in the local mall. My toddler had a meltdown and was doing that high-pitched scream that makes ears bleed. Yes, I think you know the sound.

As I was trying to manage a stressful moment, an elderly woman looked over at us and shook her head in disgust. I had to take her to task on it because I have a low tolerance for passive-aggressive communication. I wanted her to say the words she was obviously thinking: That my kid was out of control and I was a terrible parent. I wanted her to stand by her dirty looks. I wanted her to own it, and I would have been fine with that (not really, but still!). When I asked her why she was shaking her head, she stood by them alright, informing me that I should do a better job of "training" him. I almost had a temper tantrum myself at that point.

I suggested that if she found it too noisy, perhaps a café rather than a mall food court might better suit. Another suggestion I offered was that she come to my house and reform my entire collection of unruly children, teaching me a few parenting lessons along the way. Finally, I suggested that she consider lending a hand to an exhausted mother struggling with small children instead of judging me. But Mrs. McJudgerson offered no help—only criticism.

When the food court spectacle came to an end, another elderly woman made her way over to us to reach out with support and understanding. She explained to me that people like that are not worth a second thought. Her kindness turned my anger into sadness; my lip began to quiver, then came a quiet tear, then another.

Why was I so sad? I was confused at first.

I was sad because the first woman I encountered was the reason so many mamas are stressed out with worry that they are doing a bad job as parents. She was the reason mamas feel too overwhelmed to take their small children on outings. She was the reason mamas get trapped at home, socially isolated—they are afraid of going out there and being judged. And this type of mommy culture needs to stop.

I was also upset because I was worried about that toddler of mine. His tantrums were extreme because his language was so delayed. I was scared of having to travel down the autism road for a second time—a trip I really didn't want to have to take—and it felt like this woman was rubbing my face in it. I specifically took my little one there because I was trying to program and practice doing outings with him. I was concerned about his development so I was creating situations and teachable moments. I was being a good mom, and yet someone attempted to make me feel like a bad mom. The real lesson is that we never really know what is going on in the lives of others.

We mamas have to stick together and commit to not letting the Judgy McJudgersons' voices silence ours. We will continue to take our kids on outings and refuse to listen to any parenting poison. Most of all, when we see each other struggling, we will offer help and under-standing—without judgment. As parents, we need to come together in support and understanding. There is no space for judgment and shame.

Let's show up kindly for each other. Build your own "Mabelhood" on a foundation of support, compassion, and kindness. You will never go wrong. And if you see another mom being bullied, shamed, or criticized anywhere, stand up and step up. Lend your voice and show her you have her back. That is how we build strong communities.

BUSINESS, BABIES, AND MOTHERHOOD ARE LIKE AN ONGOING HORMONE CYCLE

Driving this mothership while raising all six of my kids and helping grow and run a business can make me feel like I'm running with my head cut off some days. Now imagine that, times double, when experiencing some tweenage hormone rage!

The other day, I was picking up my daughters from dance class, and I was greeted by some stressed out mothers who had recently been experiencing a bit of "tween girl hormonal rage." Considering the ages of my girls, she was seeking my advice. While I think I've gotten off pretty easily in the hormonal attitude department, I do have a few tricks up my sleeve that are worth sharing, that you can apply within motherhood, your relationships, or even your business:

1) **Make sure they get sleep**. Big kids may resent little kid bedtimes, but they need them. For years, I had one kiddo bedtime at my house as it applied to everyone from toddler to tween. I don't like kid meltdowns at any age, and sleep is a good way to prevent them.

2) **Make sure you get some sleep too.** I believe that sleep cures most things—heartache, conflict, stress, and so many other health benefits! I know it's tempting to do the work grind in the night once the kids are asleep, but give yourself at least a night or two off from your work routine, so you can unwind, get in bed early, and catch some zzzs too!

3) **Don't stoop to their level**. I mean it. Do not stoop to tween level, toddler level, or even raging adult level. Maintain a calm and cool head. Take a deep breath and stop yourself from getting into a screaming match and door-slamming competition with your moody teens and tweens. The same goes when somebody angers you in business or life situations. You will only escalate the situation by getting sucked into it.

4) **Don't take their crap**. Or anyone's for that matter. Just because they have raging hormones and may lack some self-control, it doesn't mean you have to take their verbal abuse. Expect to be spoken to with respect. Mouthy kids need a break to compose themselves and cool off. And mouthy adults, well, send them love and compassion, and cut them right out. After stating your piece, of course.

5) **Talk to them**. Once they've chilled out a bit, you can have a productive chat and explain why the way they acted is not acceptable in the family. Chances are they feel bad for how

they behaved even if they are stubborn in admitting it. Apply the same principle at work or in your business.

6) **Keep talking to them**. Was there a trigger? Hold space and witness them. There might be some bigger issues going on. Did they get in a fight with a friend at school? Are they worried about a math test? Provide many opportunities throughout the day for open conversations. You never know what little tidbits might get leaked! In your business, or within your life, take it a step further and have a mini coffee chat with your team—everyone if possible. Create an open and safe space for them to share their thoughts and concerns. It's how you grow together—as a family.

The most important thing I tell myself is to *never ever take anything they or anyone says personally!* Remember your own experience, that moment in your early twenties you realized your parents were human—*gasp!*—and had these things called *feelings* and they actually did so much for you? Yeah, it'll happen. You just have a decade of exercising extreme patience ahead of you before it does.

If you can master your emotional intelligence and cultivate patience along with active listening skills, I really do believe you can conquer the world—at least the world of tweenage hormones and any other rage-y adults who haven't yet mastered theirs.

PARENTING DURING A PANDEMIC

The issue of having kids home all the time while trying to work really tried everyone's patience during the pandemic. Our kids were home trying to stay focused with online schooling, while most of us shifted to working from home full time. It was a struggle for so many.

I was fortunate that for my family, our time in lockdown wasn't as problematic as it was for some. For us, it provided a wonderful opportunity to slow down, connect, and remind us of what is truly important in life. But I understand that enjoying this time comes from a place of privilege for me. My kids are older and able to take care of themselves. I didn't have to worry about losing my job. We've been at Mabel's Labels long enough to be able to pivot easier than a lot of businesses. Having a virtual store, with no brick-and-mortar building, meant that we were always open for customers through our website.

While so many people were posting pictures of their treasured family time, I was astutely aware that this time was only wonderful for those who did not have to worry about the circumstances that many people were living with every day. The lockdowns were incredibly difficult for many. And to those people, I want to say that I see you:

- If you were having to homeschool and feel accountable to multiple teachers, while also being accountable to your boss and report about your productivity. It would suck having to spend your days "shushing" your kids for Zoom meetings, while juggling their responsibilities as well.

- If you have really little kids, not being able to take babies and toddlers to play groups, nursery school, the park, or to visit Grandma is incredibly isolating.
- If the money earners in your family have been laid off or you are without income.
- If you have a child with disabilities and there is no more speech therapy, occupational therapy, and PSWs providing needed services to your family.
- If you are a single parent who has an unreliable co-parent and you are carrying the full load.
- If you live in a home that is toxic or are stuck in the house with an abusive or disengaged partner.

Again, the shutdowns were relatively easy for me. I have a lot of kids, so they have built-in friends to swim and play games with while staying at home. No one here lost a job. But occasionally, when I would go to post some of the fun on social media, I would pause and think about how this might land on some of the parents I've acknowledged above. Let's all be kind and remember that not everyone is in the same situation. As the saying goes, "We're all in the same storm, but not the same boat."

Parents of teens are discovering the unique challenges isolation presents for this age group. So far, I'm surviving the outrageous amounts of teen hormones, constant snacking, sleeping until all hours, and occasional eye rolls. There are a few reminders I have to give myself:

1) **They're kind of sad and that's fair.** I have a kid in Grade 8 whose school play, graduation trip, and graduation ceremony got canceled. I've got another one in her last year of high school. No prom for her. My university kids were sent home and are missing going to lectures and hanging out with their friends. Sure, the teens are healthy and we are grateful for that, but we need to honor the loss they are feeling. They are missing out on important events.

2) **Encourage teens to create a schedule and stick to it.** I find the teens are happier and feel more accomplished when they set some goals and accomplish them. Have them make their own schedule—they will be more invested in something they create. Be sure to encourage some physical activity as well.

3) **Love in the time of COVID.** If you have a teen with a budding romance, try to empathize with them. Remember the thrill that first time you met someone who made your heart skip a beat? Remember how you wanted to be together at all times? Your teen is missing that person so hard right now. Don't minimize their feelings. You may see it as puppy love, but to them, this is the real deal and a very significant relationship.

4) **Get involved in their activities.** So maybe creating TikToks and learning the latest video game is not really your jam. It doesn't have to be. But by participating in something that is important to them, you're sending them a big message of love.

5) **Parents unite.** Our teens think we are the only mean parents out there who are insisting on sticking to the physical distancing rules. Let's all commit to doing a very good job of sticking to the rules so that we can all be the meanest parents in the world together. Parents of teens everywhere must be consistent.

Living through a pandemic is a very tricky time for all parents. No one is getting off easy here, including parents of teens. If you're dealing with a grumpy door-slamming kid who is saying awful things to you, just remember to stick to the golden rule of parenting teens: do not take anything they say personally. And keep your eye on the prize—you will get them out of your house eventually!

But as the lockdowns lift and life returns to normal or a semi-normal state, old parenting problems resurface, like balancing kids and work in the summer. Working mothers everywhere groan as summer approaches for the simple reason that while school is out, work is not. Summer represents the ultimate juggling act for working parents as we try to manage spending time with our kids while fulfilling our professional responsibilities. On top of the inconvenience, summers can be expensive when you take into account childcare costs.

- Juggling holidays. One option is for both parents to take separate holidays so each can cover kiddo duty while off work. Trading off can be a smart financial move, but it does sometimes mean that the family has to forgo a family holiday together. An easy solution can be keeping things simple. If the working parent can take a long weekend occasionally, it allows for a family to do a local activity or even have a fun and cheap staycation. There's nothing wrong with staying home as a family, turning the sprinkler on and having a barbeque!

- Camp Grandma. Do you have a retired family member who might like a visit from your little darlings? Intergenerational fun is valuable for many reasons. Getting to spend time with an older relative is great for kids, and it provides parents with an affordable solution for part of the summer. Not everyone has this option, so if you do, take advantage of it!

- Hire a student. If you have school-aged kids, you don't necessarily need a childcare professional. If you can hire a competent and fun high school or college student, they will provide your kiddos with endless fun at a reasonable price. You may not come home to a tidy house or dinner in the oven, but many parents are just happy to see their kids having a great summer, which can mean crafts everywhere and kids covered in dirt!

- Work for a company that is results focused, which allows for more flexibility for employees to spend time with their families as long as their goals are met and work is complete.

Balancing kids and work during the summers or even during the pandemic over the last two years hasn't been easy. Working parents have had to get creative. Many, myself included, are all working from home. Being stuck at home has caused many moms to look around and say, "Where did all this stuff come from?" And I get it. We are in each other's spaces and faces more than ever. You're not alone in wanting to organize your space, minimize clutter, and just keep the house as minimalistic as possible. I'm no exception, and I've learned a few little tricks along the way that can help you both manage your workload as well as organize your home:

EAT THE FROG

This concept is something I apply to my worklife. The expression refers to doing the job you least like first thing in the morning. When the most-dreaded job is done, you don't spend the whole day obsessing about it or procrastinating. It's also a great way to approach home organization. Which job have you been dreading the most? Is it cleaning that junk drawer? Is it dealing with those toiletries that have been under your sink for a decade? Eat that frog, Mama!

LOSE THAT SENTIMENTAL FEELING

I know we want to hold on to every craft, drawing, and report card that enters our homes. Here's the thing: the longer you hold onto that stuff, the harder it is to toss it! With six kids and lots of "stuff," I've had to be ruthless, with a full recycling box every week. Every time I see my own mother, she's handing me boxes of my junk she held onto. What am I going to do with my Grade 3 report card?! I'm saving my kids the hassle of having it land on them when they're adults. If you can't bring yourself to clear out the crafts, you can always take a picture of it and start a file on your computer. That's much more space efficient.

SPACE IS MORE VALUABLE THAN STUFF

My grandma raised a very big family in a very small house, and this was her philosophy. I live in a big house and there is a definite down-side—however much space you have, you *will* fill it. Try to fight that mentality. I've challenged myself to try to ignore that basement and all the storage space so that it doesn't become a dumping ground of procrastination!

One in, three out

In trying to declutter, I've told my kids that when something new comes in the house, three things must leave. When they were young, it was toys, and now that they're teenagers, it's hoodies. Why must they want so many hoodies?

The problem with donating

A lot of organizations have stopped accepting donations right now. Don't let that deter you from organizing. Collect your bags and put them out of the way. If you have a garage or basement, store them there. One day, these organizations that need donations will be so happy to take those bags off your hands.

If your organizing or balancing act isn't going so well, don't sweat it! We've got loads of time, and when you've got small children under foot, it's hard to get anything done. Some days, we might be super productive, and other days, not so much. These times call for guilt-free parenting, so go easy on yourselves!

#bizhack

"You don't have to attend every argument you're invited to." –Unknown

#lifehack

"Dust if you must, but the world's out there, with the sun in your eyes, the wind in your hair . . . And when you go, go you must—you yourself, will make more dust."
–Rose Milligan

#momhack

Don't pay your kids to do chores (or feel guilty for asking). They are not "helping" you, they are family members who must contribute to the running of the household. Family is a community that comes with responsibilities.

chapter eight

Family Core Values

We all have a code we live by, things we hold sacred. Values we like to uphold in our lives, in our families, and at our workplace. Values we build our brands and business on, otherwise known as core values. At some point a few years ago, we went through an extensive exercise at work identifying and defining our core values. It made sense to me that our family should discuss and establish our core values as well. These are the basic things we can all agree on that will make our family culture not only function, but thrive.

For years, I had our core values scribbled on a piece of paper and pinned to a corkboard in the house. But recently, a talented friend created a much more beautiful way to display our family core values. These are ours:

- Be organized.
- Use good manners.
- Be a peacekeeper.

- Be a good listener.
- Be helpful without being asked.
- Talk it over.
- Use your cool voice.
- Be quick to forgive.
- Remember always: The people who love you the most in the world live in this house. Be patient and appreciative.

What is not posted is something we often talk about. We call it "The Code." This has to do with any confidential information you receive as a result of being a member of the family. This information cannot be shared. It is generally embarrassing in nature. The kind of things included in The Code would be:

- Never reveal a sibling's crush in public.
- Never, no matter how angry you might be at a sibling, reveal information such as the child be a bed wetter, they are afraid of the dark, etc.
- Never, and I mean NEVER say something so mean when you're in a fight that no matter how much you apologize, the person who is on the receiving end will never be able to FORGET what was said to them. Usually these kinds of comments would be directly insulting their appearance or personality. In other words, you always FIGHT FAIR.

It's so important to be kind to those you love and live with because life outside of the home isn't always a friendly and supportive place. We all have stories from our childhood or youth of bullies and mean people who for some reason took pleasure in making someone miserable. Who remembers the movie *Mean Girls*? For many, it brought back some uncomfortable memories. As a parent, it also made me think about my daughters and whether they'd ever experienced such mean-spirited and petty behavior.

We've all heard the term "mean girls." It refers to the notion that tween and teen girls are exclusive and irrationally mean to one another. I find the term is bothersome—any generalizations, particularly when they target young women, make me feel twitchy.

Sure, I've heard some stories, and I know that friendship, emotions, social lives, and defining one's place in the world are all complicated issues for young people. Sometimes along the journey, kids find themselves acting in a way that might not reflect the kind of person they will be once they mature.

Honestly, in my experience of raising daughters, we have not personally encountered "mean girl" situations. None of them have had a lot of friendship drama, issues with exclusivity, or experienced general "mean girl" attitudes from their friends and peers.

This led to reflect on *why* maybe we've been able to avoid this drama that we hear and read so much about.

- **Role modeling.** My girls don't see me act petty or gossip about people. I don't speak badly of my friends or other women. I try to role model good behavior. Children don't do as they're told, they do as they see, which is why being mindful of our behavior goes a long way. This parenting gig is all about the role modeling. Don't waste your time telling them how to act, show them how to act with your own words and actions.

- **Resilience.** I find that if my girls have a problem with a kid, they share their feelings about how the behavior made them feel with said kid and move on without holding a grudge. Perhaps that is a result of being a part of a big family. We HAVE to deal with our issues and move on in our family. We couldn't function otherwise—there's many people, too many personalities, and too much room for conflict in our household. Perhaps my girls have generalized that skill with their social groups outside of the home. I've also noticed that if a kid does not behave in a way that my daughters approve of, they are not desperate to gain that kid's acceptance or approval. They simply move on to their other friends. They don't try to hang out with kids who don't want to hang out with them.

- **Kindness is our currency.** If my girls do tell me about a child at school who is not acting kindly to others, I remind them that something is likely going on with that kid, at home or otherwise, that is making them feel vulnerable and insecure. Their behavior may be reflecting that. We need to be patient, but also speak out and self-advocate.

I'm pretty sure there are many mothers out there, including yourself, doing these same things, yet have kids who seem to attract drama and conflict in their social situations. It happens, so don't beat yourself up, or your child for that matter. It will likely pass quickly.

It's not easy to always navigate conflict and drama; it does a number on the nervous system, and worse, it diminishes self-confidence and self-worth, especially when not handled in a healthy manner. We could all take it upon ourselves to be a little kinder to one another—in how we speak to each other, navigate conflict, manage our emotions—and in turn show our kids that kindness really is the cool way to act. We can create a ripple effect that lasts for a lifetime.

#bizhack

"World domination is a full-time job!" Posted on the wall at Mabel's Labels HQ

#lifehack

"A mom who has big dreams outside her family is still the same mom who has big dreams for her family." –Alyssa DeRose (and every other mom entrepreneur everywhere)

#momhack

You are free to pivot, shift, and birth the life that you always wanted. Choose you, Mama. Because when you choose you, everything else aligns.

chapter nine

Women Have Communities—
Find Yours

My grandmother was one of twenty-one children and gave birth to nine herself. So you may find it odd that I was extremely nervous to tell her about my last few pregnancies. I come from a prolific family, so you may wonder why I felt on edge about breaking more baby news to my elderly grandmother. Quite simply, it was because she's a strange combination of a traditional Irish Catholic mother mixed with an intellectual feminist—picture Gloria Steinem as the mother on *Little House on the Prairie*.

While she outwardly greeted my pregnancy news with joy, her eyes cried out: "Why so many children when you women now have CHOICE, Julie?" Okay, it wasn't so much with her eyes, but with her mouth. Grandma was a straight shooter!

And so begins the trip down memory lane. I remind myself what her life was like when she raised children. They were new to Canada, and her husband worked two jobs, which meant she was single-handedly running a household and virtually housebound. In addition, the women of her generation were so bogged down with the daily tasks of running a household that there was barely time to even enjoy their children. Those were the days when a woman's status could be tied to if she was the first to have her cloth diapers drying on the clothesline each morning.

We can agree that as much as we love our children, motherhood can be an isolating and mind-numbing task at times. It really is no wonder that Grandma shakes her head and asks why a woman of my age and in these times would choose to have six children.

There are several glaring differences to the lives of mothers now and the lives of our foremothers, most notably the internet. Even on those days when we can't escape the four walls of our noisy households and we feel the walls are closing in on us, the internet opens us up to a community of support, and a break from the monotony of raising children.

We blog and read blogs. We connect on Facebook groups. We share Instagram reels and may even have some fun on TikTok. If at 3:00 a.m. you're wondering why your toddler has green poops, you can post it on a mama message board knowing that by 4:00 a.m. you will likely have several responses, including some that simply reach out to say they understand your stress. During the loneliest hours of motherhood, simply logging on to your computer can be your virtual savior. I know it was mine. Don't underestimate the power of online communities. People mock online friendships and support groups, but they are real. During these uncivilized years of raising kids, you do whatever needs to be done to keep the sanity. Sometimes that means hopping onto a bit of technology and connecting to all the other mamas out there.

Do what you need to do to ensure that you don't feel alone. It might mean venturing into your neighborhood café or befriending the moms at school or at swimming lessons. It might mean being a part of a gazillion and one Facebook groups—who cares?! Create your lifeline and call on them for support when you need it. We need adult friendships, especially as we dive deeper and deeper into the journey that is motherhood and entrepreneurship. And even more so when you are a mom of a kid with special needs. Having a community provides a feeling of comfort and safety, and it allows you to witness yourself and others on this wild and crazy journey!

And if you are feeling left out, or have been to the lion's share of online communities and not found one that you can totally feel a part of, create your own. Be the change you were searching for in the first place. Shine your light, bright and strong. Share your story and your journey through a blog post, a podcast interview, or a simple good old Instagram or Facebook post. You'll be surprised just how quickly you attract those who either expand you, activate you, or ground you. Being a mom is hard, and sometimes you need to connect, listen, share, vent, or even roar.

Ever seen how a lioness or even a mama bear protects her cubs? She is fierce. Nobody dare question her litter, or even glance at her cubs the wrong way. The same should apply to us as mamas, but for some reason, we often tend to people please, over explain, and do all sorts of things that give away our power. And here's the thing: sometimes you gotta bring out the cheekiness. You gotta bring out the roar.

My roars have been clipped, succinct, and very direct. For instance, when people see, hear, or realize that you have six children, many questions and comments follow. Here's a list of the ones I most commonly hear, including a few of my favorite answers:

Question/comment: "Why did you have so many kids?"
My response: "I kept having them until I had one I liked."

Question/comment: "You look really good. For having had six kids."
My response: "Put a period after the word 'good' and say no more."

Question/comment: "You don't look like you've had six kids."
(Said while their eyes go up and down my body.)
My response: "You can't see my uterus."

Question/comment: "So, is this a blended family?"

My response: "I'm not sure how that is relevant, but it just so happens the children have the same genetic contributors."

Question/comment: "Are they ALL yours?!"

My response: "Look at this T-shirt."

Question/comment: "So, are you DONE?"

My response: "I'll let you know after I pee on a stick tomorrow morning."

And every single time, the above or similar questions have been asked, you might as well picture a dignified, but very ferocious roar coming from me. I get it; most people ask because they are genuinely interested in a family that is quite different from theirs.

You see, I had my first baby when I was in my late twenties. It felt young at the time because I never fancied myself as having babies that early in life. I just had too much to do and didn't really need a baby slowing me down. Turns out it didn't slow me down much at all. Regardless, a baby at that age was not something I would have predicted for myself. And as the number of babies I had increased, so did the number of candles on my birthday cake. Having babies a little later in life is getting more and more common.

The issue of maternal age has always been a discussion point. In days gone by, the older mother was frowned upon. My grandmother gave birth for the last time at the age of forty-six and was subjected to, what I consider, verbal abuse while she was at the hospital delivering the baby. A nurse scolded her, insisting that Grandma should be "ashamed" of herself. And there was the issue of the embarrassment she caused some of her adult and teenaged children.

While those social stigmas may no longer apply, maternal age is still relevant. Somewhere between my fourth and fifth pregnancy, I reached the magical age of thirty-five years old. Apparently, it all goes downhill for pregnant women and their fetuses from there. I began receiving the elderly treatment: amniocentesis offered around every corner, suggestions of a tubal legation during the C-section since clearly another baby was out of the question. It seemed odd to me since I had been pregnant with my fourth child only a few months earlier. Apparently, my thirty-five candles put me into a whole new statistical category that is intended to scare the faint-hearted mamas.

Here's the thing: If you are healthy, if you have a desire to continue growing your family and are willing to go down that path—which I fully acknowledge is unique to each of our bodies, as we each have our own fertility journey—power to you and yours! Don't let ageism get to you. Go in knowing what you want, what any of your risks are, and what is best for your family. You are the expert in that department.

It's one thing not to be bothered by becoming an older mother, but another entirely when you have to surround yourself with young mothers. I had my sixth baby the year my baby cousins were having their first babies. I was like the old hag mom at family reunions. And then when that baby started school? I was invited to his friend's mom's thirtieth birthday! I was already well into my forties by that time. I was the token mom who was sporting crow's feet and whose biggest bragging point was that I had had one, two, or three kids in diapers for twelve years, four months, and twenty-six days straight. How's that for a flex?!

Many people are fascinated when they find out that I am a mom of six and I run a successful business. They are curious to know why six kids? Was it the plan? Is it a religious thing? Here's the truth: I don't have the "I'm done" gene. Let me explain what I mean. My thoughts were always: *One baby at a time and see how it goes.*

Our unique situation was that our eldest child, Mack, was diagnosed with autism when he was three. Many think we are brave for having more kids because there was likely a genetic predisposition putting our future children in the higher-risk category of having autism. Did I want to go down the autism road a second time? Not particularly, but at least I'd know what to do. There were many advantages to having a lot of siblings for my son. He was socialized all the time. Someone was always dragging him into imaginative play, and his deficits were addressed as a matter of necessity all day long. His gains have been remarkable, and I don't doubt the role his siblings have played in that. So did I have them just to help Mack? Clearly not; I already had three kids when he was diagnosed. But it is an awesome bonus. We love our babies and having a big family, and the added bonus is that it has helped him so much. Also note, that while we expected Mack to go to university and have relationships and live entirely independently, when you do have a lot of children and also a child with a disability, it's quite nice to know for future planning. Long and short, yes, autism is scary, but for us the advantages of having more kids outweigh the risks. SO that is the answer to the question of WHY we have six kids. And I wouldn't change anything for the world.

I've often been shocked when people hand me over their maternity clothes and baby gear after their second or third baby. *How are they so sure they won't need it again?* These mama friends have all assured me that they *knew* they were done. After my last couple of babies, I realized that maybe some of us never get that feeling of being done. I expected it after my fourth, fifth, and definitely my sixth. Never happened. I describe myself as having missed out on the "I'm done" gene. Every time I have a baby, I expect to be greeted with a satisfied feeling of baby closure, an urge to close up shop for this tired uterus once and for all. Well, I'm still waiting.

I'm guessing that it's that same gene that allows women to purge their maternity clothes, pack up the bassinet, and happily send husbands off for a minor surgical procedure. For those of us not blessed with the gene, we find each of those actions baffling. How do those women just know?

Having a big family is a choice that we made. The realities are that we just really enjoyed babies and our mentality was that we're already used to not sleeping through the nights and packing up a lot of things whenever we went somewhere anyway, so why not.

WHAT YOU CAN EXPECT WHEN YOU HAVE A BIG FAMILY:

- **Comments, lots of comments.** "Don't you have a TV?" and "Are they ALL yours?" They're usually surprised that there's not at least one set of twins in the mix because who would ever chose to have that many kids!

- **Staring.** We get stared at wherever we go. Can't walk from one end of the mall to the other, and if we go to a restaurant, we get a lot of looks. A table for eight is usually for a group celebration, but for us it's simply for a family dinner out. And when we get on a plane, people look shocked and scared that we'll be in their section.

- **Judgments and assumptions.** People have opinions about your fertility. People thought I was running a daycare out of my house. One friend from Ottawa came over with her two-year-old and the kid asked if this was her new daycare.

THINGS YOU NEED TO CONSIDER:

- **Expenses.** I'm a believer that kids are as expensive as you make them, within reason. But we are going to have six kids going off to university one after the next, and we have to plan for that. We put a lot of cash into our RESPs. We had to plan for that expense.

- **How would you navigate motherhood if you didn't have the perfect baby?** Are you going to be able to manage if you have a child with a disability? What if you do have twins? You get what you get and we can't socially engineer what baby we're going to have.

- **No more me time or date night.** These things just don't happen! The last manicure I had was for my wedding day, and I've had one massage in my life and I spent the whole time thinking about all the things I could be getting done. When I get my hair cut and highlighted, I leave with it wet because I don't even have time for a blow-dry. My me time standard is totally different from most. If I can do something with just a couple of them, it feels like me time. As for date night, six is too many kids to ask your mother to watch, and it's a two babysitter job, which makes it cost prohibitive.

- **How are you with no sleep?** If you love your zzzs, this is going to be hard. I have mamas who tell me they had a bad night, then they describe it to me and it sounds like one of my better nights! And with baby after baby, there are consecutive years of not sleeping properly.

- **How are you with mess and chaos?** If you keep your house impeccably clean, then don't bother having all these kids because you will be SO busy keeping the place tidy that you'll never have time to spend with them. You also better not have a thing against doing laundry. We usually do two to three loads a day, every day. I don't worry about the house so much. I have a high threshold for chaos, and it shows. I'm a mama of many, not a maid to many!

- **Are you a complainer?** If so, don't bother because you will complain and NO one will care or listen to you.

- **Are you going to get frazzled with every sniffle?** When you have a lot of kids, there's a lot of sickness. Someone's always got something! Chicken pox, lice, pink eye, stomach flu, diarrhea, puking, sniffles, fever . . . something. Always something!

- **Can you handle the bickering?** Man, that's exhausting. I've had to pull over the van on so many outings and reshuffle booster seats. Everything has to be planned strategically to keep the bickering to a minimum.

- **How are your pregnancies?** Some people say pregnancy is addictive because of all the attention you get. I can assure you, when you have had numerous pregnancies, you get NO special attention. I was lugging ski gear around one winter, taking care of everyone and everything. You actually forget you are pregnant because you're so busy. And everyone else forgets too! My last baby was a spring baby and I completely forgot to tell people, like the other moms at school and nursery school. When my winter coat came off, they were like, "Uh, when are you due?" Oops, next week!

THE TRICKY TRANSITIONS

People always wonder, what is the hardest leap. Going from one to two kids or from five to six, but it's completely individual. It's also amazing how your perspective and perceptions change. I remember after my fifth C-section, the two older ones went away with their dad overseas to visit family, and I was left with a three-year-old, a toddler, and a newborn. Everyone asked if I was enjoying my holiday with just three kids! Everything is relative!

I'm going to say that most find transitioning from having your first baby to the second is the hardest. I think parents find it difficult because they were able to give their first baby so much love and attention. It's a guilt double whammy for many—they feel guilty for their older child who is suddenly dethroned and now has to WAIT for the first time ever, and they feel guilty for the newborn who doesn't get the same undivided attention that their sibling got.

Sure, going to three switches you from the man-to-man defense to the zone defense, but you've likely got a slightly older kid then who might be in nursery school or at least has a bit of common sense, which makes it easier. The one notable memory about once the third arrived was it seemed like the laundry tripled. It went to laundry every day with baby number three.

I found going from four to five a little tricky, mostly because when my fifth was born, my eldest child was only six. It was a lot of small humans, and even if one or two were not there, it was still busy. Going to the fifth brought some practical issues as well, like needing a bigger vehicle. Another vehicle change happened again when our sixth baby arrived.

GETTING THROUGH THE DAY

Learn to triage the situation. I know you are spread very thin and everything seems to be a top priority, but you need to be realistic: bleeding child gets dealt with first, hungry child second, whining annoying child last. But they get it. They know they have to be patient, and maybe a little more independent. And they get that they have to help each other out because Mama only has two hands.

People always wonder how I give them all the love and attention they need. The love is easy. You really do keep falling in love with them, one after the other. As for attention, each kid has different requirements. Know your kids. Some require one-on-one time, some don't. My mother always said, "You don't treat your kids the same because they're NOT the same." You get to know what and when they need something. They're different kids and often have different wants and needs. And what they lack in attention from me, I feel they get from each other. And when I say lack of attention, I mean I don't act as their servant. I have seen my kids' friends bark orders at their mothers—"Get me a glass of milk"—and I want to shout, "Get off your eight-year-old ass and get your own glass of milk!"

Use the tricks:

- Take the day in twenty-minute chunks. Thinking too far ahead may overwhelm you.

  - Plan nap times and activities strategically. I manipulated nap times and activities to give me times of day when I got some peace and quiet and was able to get work done.

  - Find help if you need it. When I had kids needing to go to the bus stop in the middle of winter, but also three small babes at home, I organized a neighborhood kid to come to the house every day and walk them to the bus stop. My little bus buddy was a lifesaver. As she got older, she also became a homework helper as well.

- Carpool. I'm a big fan of carpooling and even post on my neighborhood moms' Facebook group to do a callout about whose kids are doing what activities in hopes of finding some driving pals!

- Don't freak out if it's been a rough day. In fact, take this as an opportunity to let yourself off the hook and order pizza.

- Don't over worry about sibling jealousy. I actually never witnessed an older sibling showing resentment about the arrival of a new baby.

- All age gaps between siblings has pros and cons, but I loved having mine close together. I was already in that baby headspace. And with any luck, I figured they'd keep each other busy being playmates. That worked out, but I kind of forgot the toll listening to them bicker would take!

GETTING OUT THE DOOR

I clearly run a busy household. Many moms have asked me for advice on how to deal with the stress and anxiety of getting everyone ready and out the door on time in the morning.

It's been an ongoing learning process for me—a process that hit its peak around the time our fifth kiddo arrived. My oldest son was six and attending school full days. His two younger siblings, ages three and four (at the time) were in junior and senior kindergarten, respectively. It meant I had to have three kids ready to catch the school bus by 7:45 a.m. every day, while juggling a newborn and seventeen-month-old. The challenges were countless. Our Canadian winters provided further complications with the additional step of putting on snowsuits and boots. To add to the pressure, I was doing it on my own since Daddy-o left for work right around the time the children were waking up.

When I had all six, I had to get four young kids ready and off to school every day, while still having two at home getting under foot in the mornings. So what have I learned about keeping my sanity while maintaining my record of never having a child miss the school bus?

GOT A BABY?

If the baby needs a feed while you are getting children out the door, it is game over. Try to manipulate the baby's feeding schedule so that you are free for a half hour before takeoff time.

LET THE LITTLE THINGS GO

So maybe your toddler and baby have to sit in their nighttime diaper a little longer than you'd like, but get those big kids out the door before dealing with the little ones. I don't think there are any studies to indicate that sitting in a diaper for an extra half hour in the morning causes any long-term damage.

PREP THE NIGHT BEFORE

This is obvious, but I mean really prep. Clothes laid out, cereal on the table, backpacks packed, lunches made. Anything that can be done in advance, do it. If you ever find yourself saying, "Oh, I'll just do that in the morning," promptly tell yourself to shut up and go and get it done.

DON'T LET CHILDREN MAKE CHOICES IN THE MORNING

I know this sounds harsh, but if you start asking everyone what they want for breakfast, you'll soon turn into a short-order cook. Serve up one breakfast item to all. Keep it simple—go with cereal and fruit if you can get away with it.

TRAIN FOR INDEPENDENCE

I had a "Before School Plan" poster hanging up in my hallway. There were two sections. The first section outlined everything the children had to do in the morning: get dressed, go to the bathroom, eat breakfast, brush teeth, etc. The second section was a backpack checklist to make sure they had everything they needed for the day: lunch, water bottle, library books, gym shoes, etc. You can personalize yours to your child's routine. My kids found the visual cue very helpful as a reminder to self-evaluate how far along they were in getting ready. If you've got a non-reader, do it with pictures. I also had an "After School Plan," which instructed them to put their agendas in their in-trays, put their lunch boxes on the kitchen counter, etc.

FIND YOURSELF A "SECRET WEAPON"

For years, my secret weapon was a neighborhood kid we called Miss Nicole. She came to the house fifteen minutes before the bus arrived, helped with any last minute issues, then walked them to the bus stop and supervised them on the bus. She returned them home at the end of the day as well. She was a huge help! It saved me from bundling up the little ones and standing in subzero temperatures waiting for a school bus. The few bucks I threw at Miss Nicole each week was money well spent.

If you also have to get yourself out the door and presentable in a timely fashion, the only way to do it is to wake up half an hour before the children to get yourself ready. With a little patience, organization, and a master plan, mornings don't have to be filled with anxiety. And it's hard for anyone to have a happy and productive day when it starts off with a lot of stress.

#bizhack

Use all of the resources available to you. There are programs, grants, and mentors all out there waiting for you. Do your research and never stop asking questions.

#lifehack

"Please go find a sibling to play with. It's why we had them." Me, tongue in cheek. Kind of.

#momhack

Your kids have different needs so don't treat them the same. Parents often feel guilty for treating their kids differently, but their kids ARE different. Equal does not always equate to fair.

chapter ten

Boundaries and Connections

My lovely grandmother passed away at the age of 101, and she'd given birth to a lot of babies. She had babies in the 1930s, 40s, 50s, and 60s. She was collecting the government offered "baby bonus" and old-age pension at the same time! Grandma was as wise as she was old, so when she spoke, this humble creator of six babies dropped everything and listened.

Grandma once shared that she thought women should not gather and talk about their kids. Huh? That's right. At first, I found this to be a very strange perspective. I have six kids and can turn every conversation into a discussion around their accomplishments, challenges, teachers, activities, poops, pukes, and sleeping patterns. What more was there going on in my life? If not for gabbing about my kiddos, what else could I say? Like, who am I without my children? Mabel's Labels was even inspired because of one of them.

That was precisely her point. I once returned from a weekend away with my longtime girlfriends. You know the kind of gals I'm talking about—the ones who have been around since the beginning of time. They were there holding your hair back while you puked up the peach schnapps you guzzled in the school parking lot before the dance. They remember when you got your driver's license, cried with you that first time your heart was broken, and would share your single dorm room bed during a weekend visit at university. These are the gals who were your bridesmaids and actually knew what you were like before you were someone's mom.

The weekend was geared to be a fantastic catch-up with the old gang, and Grandma gave me strict instructions to report back to her with all the gossip and antics the weekend held. However, come Monday morning, the two of us sat with our cups of tea and I delivered a shockingly boring report. I walked away from that weekend knowing that little Johnny was an exceptional reader and little Janey was the best player on her soccer team, but I didn't know much else.

Lamenting this, my grandma perked up and told me it was time to implement "The Rule."

What rule, you ask? Hold your wine or coffee or whatever. As a young mother, Grandma occasionally gathered with a group of women. It was one of the very rare occasions they did not have their children with them. She set a rule for the group that no one was permitted to even whisper their child's name. "The Rule" was complied with, and these women enjoyed many years of social gatherings, discussing every topic imaginable—except their kids.

The next year came quickly and our annual weekend together was around the corner. The emails started flying: deciding who was driving, who was cooking, who was bringing the wine! Now was the time to suggest "The Rule," but I was concerned with how it would be received. I was telling people I didn't want to hear about their kids, but the bonus was they didn't have to hear about mine!

The two childless friends immediately responded to me, thanking me profusely. I had been elevated to hero status in their eyes. The other emails started trickling in. Everyone agreed that it was time for "The Rule" to be passed on to our generation.

Listen, I'm not saying that our children aren't our world. What I'm saying is this: Before we had our children, there was a version of us who did the things we loved. Who knew how to kick back and have fun. There was a time when you prioritized yourself. I'm not saying that you shouldn't talk about your kids, you absolutely should! You, your partner, and the Big Universe/God/whatever you believe in co-created them. No one will dispute that your children are all-consuming and have a way of taking over your entire existence. Even my grandmother would readily agree. I once heard someone say having a child is like watching your heart walk around outside of your body. True enough. But every once in a while you need to step back and find that little piece of yourself that sometimes gets lost in the school meetings, hockey practices, and music lesson drop-offs. You need to find your own crown and cape and wear them for yourself. Be that for an hour every day, one day a week, or one weekend or week a year! Whatever this looks like for you, honor it and commit to "The Rule." For me, it is officially one weekend a year that I try not to let the lesson of "The Rule" stray too far.

KNOW WHEN TO SAY NO

Learning to say no can be one of the most important skills you can develop, not just as a business owner, but as a mother and a human being. All too often, we continue to feel pressured or obligated to saying yes to things when we'd rather say no. So, I'm going to ask you to practice doing this on a daily basis. I know we've got this because we actually practice saying no in our motherhood most of the time. Ice cream for dinner? No. A later bedtime? No. Not to mention saying no for things that are harmful, that can hurt someone or something, yourself included, is a good thing.

Our motto at Mabel's Labels in the early days was "Say yes and figure it out later!" It made sense at the time. As the business developed and matured, we had to be more strategic than that. Business owners need to make sure we don't get distracted by tasks and opportunities that don't actually move our business forward. Sometimes we get caught up in the weeds because we feel like we can problem solve best. The problem is, if we stay busy putting out every little brush fire, we are not thinking big enough. Say no to the brush fires. Let staff and other managers deal with them so you can be thinking about growing your business and thinking strategically. I remember having a never ending to-do list. I felt liberated when I looked at that list and turned it on its ear and into a "do not do" list. What are you doing that you could pass off to someone else? Now do just that.

I learned early in my journey that if I was going to be highly productive, I had to prioritize and say NO. I don't think it is something that women are generally good at. We end up organizing the social events at work, and we often have difficulty using this word with our children. Mine have heard my reply of: "NO is a complete sentence." When I look at the various situations when I say no, I actually realized that it was more like a YES but within my boundaries. From a professional perspective, there were several occasions when I have learned to create boundaries. As the business grew and I began doing more speaking and advising, I had countless budding entrepreneurs reach out to me for a coffee or lunch so that they could "pick my brain." I started feeling like I was an unpaid consultant; and while I like helping others, I also had my own work to do. Labels needed making and children needed raising. However, I learned so much from others in our early days that I very much felt like it was my turn to give back and share our lessons. As such, I set up a system where people who wanted to meet me could sign up for a half-hour session and meet me at a local coffee shop. I set up there and would have people come and go all morning long. Finally, I didn't feel like I was losing productivity helping everyone start their businesses because I was only designating a half day every month or so. If someone was unable to meet me during that particular day, I wouldn't bend and meet them separately, I would offer them a spot at my next coffee shop session. Putting that simple boundary in place was a game changer.

I also think it's important for people who work in offices to set up boundaries with their coworkers. We try to avoid "drive-bys" at our office. If you are busy working on a project and people keep popping in for a quick chat or piece of advice, it pulls you out of your headspace, and it often takes a few minutes to get back into what you were doing or remembering where you were. Once you settle in, the next interruption happens. Often you can finish the day without accomplishing your goals.

If this is happening to you, it might be time for a "no drive-by" policy. Of course, people can still talk to you and get your help if required, but have them email you, and you can set up a time with them that suits you. Also, don't forget to turn those notifications off, both email and social media. If you are head down in a project, be disciplined about only checking your email once every hour or two. It's when you check your email that you can respond to coworkers. Chances are, by the time you respond, they may well have solved their own problem. Remind your children and your coworkers that *"Your lack of planning does not constitute my emergency."*

I even prioritize what events I will attend. I could be at a different event every night with friends, other brands, mom groups, etc. if I always said yes. A few years ago, I only began attending conferences I was speaking at. When I do attend an event, I have a ten-point checklist that helps me decide if the event is worth my time. This is based on my professional and personal goals. Time is precious, so get the most out of yours.

Saying NO to your kids is also really helpful. I try to live by the "don't do for a child what they can do for themselves" mantra. And let's face it—there are six of them, so I simply can't do everything for them. Often when I say no, it's not mean or punishment of any kind, it's simply a natural consequence. For example, if a child forgets to bring their lunch to school, I don't drop it off to them. I could spend my life delivering forgotten items to various schools throughout my city. Not having lunch for a day is not a major problem, and they may even find their own solution by asking a sibling or a friend for an apple. Chances are, if you don't deliver a forgotten lunch to your child, they won't ever forget lunch again. I feel the same way about gym clothes, school projects, and homework. You forget your gym clothes—you sit out of gym that day. You forget a project—you get a lower mark for handing it in late. Forget your homework—maybe you have to stay in at recess to get it done. Again, none of these are used as punishment, they are just natural consequences. I've often joked with friends about that table that sits outside of the school secretary's office where parents come and drop off forgotten items. We call it "the enable table."

Same policy applies when a child comes home from school and announces they need twenty-four cupcakes for a school party the next day. When this happens, I basically look them in the eye and say, "Are you new here? Have we just met? That is NEVER going to happen." One night is not enough notice for this busy mom. Again, remember when I said "your lack of planning doesn't constitute my emergency?" This mother is not up baking all night because a child didn't provide the information earlier. Actually, let's be real—this mother isn't baking with any amount of notice, but at least a few days allows me to organize it with my local bakery. I'm very good at saying NO to baking. As my sister often jokes, "I don't make the cake; I make the money that buys the cake." Leave me to make the labels, and leave the baking to the professionals.

Giving kids the freedom to do their own problem solving is a gift to them. After all, today's problem solvers are tomorrow's leaders. They need to practice solving the smaller issues today, so that when they are older, they've had practice. No one wants to be solving problems for their adult children, but you see that happen when they have not had practice in their childhood. Also, affording my kids to problem solve on their own contributes to their growth and independence. This is very good for business; it allows me to be productive as well since my day is not getting bogged down solving every little problem that my children encounter.

Parents now even keep tabs on their kids through cell phones and tracking devices and apps. I understand there is a desire to keep kids safe and often that motivates parents to get even young children cell phones. I have resisted doing so. My experience is that there are very few true "emergencies," and when there is one I'm always located and contacted. Kids often think a cell phone emergency is to ask if they can get picked up at the mall or stay later at a friend's house. They also use phones so that parents can rescue them from a problem-solving situation. If your kids are out riding bikes and one has a fall, do they call you? My preference is for them to figure out how to get their sibling home. Maybe it means knocking on a neighbor's door to ask for assistance; maybe it means carrying the sibling home, then going back for the bike. Either way, it gives them opportunity to flex those problem-solving skills without me flying in to save the day. I like them to save their own days.

I feel similarly about tracking apps I see so many parents of teens using. Personally, I'm really not that interested in knowing where my teens are all the time. They are going to get into a bit of trouble and end up where they shouldn't. That is what happens when you are a teen and that is when you learn lessons that get carried into adulthood. Create a relationship where you can let your kids explore and have an adventure, while they feel safe enough that if something really goes wrong, they know they can count on you and that you are a safe person. Remember: raising independent kids is good for them, and will help you be more productive in both your professional and personal life.

If you're the kind of mom who gets sucked into volunteering at the school, being in charge of soccer snacks, and running the breakfast club, have a good hard look at what your volunteer priorities are and say NO to the others. Don't let yourself be "volunTOLD" into a role you are not passionate about or doesn't use your skills and talent.

I feel like busy moms always have these giant to-do lists that are basically impossible to complete. It's a good practice to create the opposite list: the do NOT do list. What are you currently doing that can be delegated to a spouse, a child, a coworker, or an assistant? You will be much more productive if you remove items from your list and only do the things that are actually important for YOU to do. An example of something on my "do not do" list is emptying the dishwasher. This is a chore my kids can do and my time is better spent attending to my children's other needs or prepping for a meeting the next day. Chores are good for kids and are not used as punishment—they are simply the tasks that have to get done for our family to function. My rule around chores is that if you get asked to do one and the response is "Why isn't (insert any sibling's name) doing that chore?" that child is immediately assigned a second chore. Another surefire way to get a second chore is to complain about the first one. Stop reading and go write your "do not do" list. I'll wait.

What are some things you can and will say no to? What are some areas in your life where boundaries can be established? You get to say yes to the things that inspire you, bring you joy, and quite frankly, make life feel a bit easy, because there's enough of everything else to go around. You don't ever have to do something you don't want to. This isn't to say that there aren't hard things that you can do and sometimes have to do. But it's high time we stopped rolling our sleeves up to do the stuff that doesn't fuel us, doesn't move the needle forward in life, business, or motherhood.

MOTIVATION MUST BE NURTURED

I've always been fascinated by what makes some people super motivated and others not so much. I found this particularly interesting when I saw differences in motivation between my children. Why do I have two kids who are equally clever, yet one is disappointed with a certain mark or grade in school, while the other thinks it is more than acceptable?

Not long ago, I spent an evening holding a gun (not literally, of course) to one kid's head forcing him to prepare for a math test taking place the next day. Across the room was the other child busily typing on her laptop. When I asked what she was working on, her response was: "I have a science test in two weeks, so I'm just putting together my study notes to get a jump on things."

Two kids, born only fifteen months apart with the same parents, same home environment, same encouragement, and same role modeling, and yet so different. Why?

With no answer to that question, frustration was mounting. When you have a smart kid not working to potential, it's enough to make any parent get twitchy. I usually rely on natural consequences: if you don't study, you fail. Better luck next time. Problem is, with this kid, doing badly doesn't bother him too much. Not exactly what I'm looking for in a consequence.

I happen to be lucky enough to be pals with psychologist and parenting author, Alyson Schafer. She gave me a few quick and helpful tips that I've put into practice, and now my kid and I are not as frustrated with each other.

Tip #1: Teach him that EFFORT IS NOT STUPIDITY. This is big. Whenever he actually had to TRY at something, he liked to default to "Oh well, I guess I just suck at this." That's a pretty easy out, so we've had lots of conversations trying to turn this way of thinking around.

Tip #2: Don't dictate when he's going to study, but task him to. Every Sunday he creates his own study plan for the week. No longer is it me nagging him to study, it's him having to be accountable to his OWN plan.

Tip #3: Don't argue when he thinks what he's studying is useless. He's likely right. Have the open conversation that there are bits of the curriculum that are outdated or won't be relevant to him. Get on his side, but remember to teach him that getting through this is all just a step to be able to have choices when it comes to post-secondary education and a career.

Keeping yourself and your team at work motivated can also be challenging. In the early days with Mabel's Labels, I was very thankful to have been accountable to my co-founders. If any of us was lacking motivation, the others helped lift each other up. We found over the years that to keep ourselves motivated and our staff, we had to do a number of things:

Tip #1: Give them time to create and play. Sometimes staff are so busy doing their job, they don't get a chance to explore and play in their field. Be sure to cut out some time for them to explore their specialty. We found this particularly important for our IT staff.

Tip #2: Invest in their professional development. It can be inspiring and motivating to attend a workshop or conference. They may meet other professionals to connect and network with, and to learn from.

Tip #3: Don't micromanage them. Watching over someone constantly and nitpicking can be very detrimental to their motivation. Give them the space to make mistakes and the grace to learn from them.

FAKING IT FOR THE KIDDOS

Who here hasn't faked something for their kids? I admit that I'm not always completely honest with my kids, but it's done in the best interests of all parties. It's not like I'm outright lying to them, more like faking it.

I fake that I like food. Don't get me wrong, I like food, but not the way most people seem to. For example, I would never in a million years cook myself something to eat. You see, the work involved is not worth the result. I'm quite happy having a bowl of cereal for dinner. But I feel like I have to be a good food role model for my kids, so I may tell them that I had soup and salad for lunch, when in reality it may have been a KitKat.

I fake that I was good at math in school. When someone asks a math trivia question, I have an easy out. I just say I don't know because I suck at math. It recently occurred to me that I don't want my kids to hear me say that. Why? Because it's an excuse not to try. Accepting how much I suck at math for years gave me a free pass from having to do anything mathematical. I don't want my kids thinking they can have free passes. Not yet. They don't think they suck at anything, and I'd like to keep it that way.

I remember when my young son asked if he could interrupt me while I was working to tell me the WHOLE back story of *Five Nights at Freddy's*. So, of course, I agreed, and my teen daughter was so impressed with how engaged and interested I looked that she recorded my reaction.

It's important to take an interest in what our kids are passionate about, regardless of how uninteresting it is to us. This is particularly true with teenagers. It's often the only way parents can keep their kids engaged and communicating with them.

It can be quite challenging to look attentive in these situations. Sometimes the glazed look comes over us, and the kids immediately turn our old trick of asking, "What did I just say?" right back at us. Of course, there isn't thing worse than getting busted. Some of my best "fake it till ya make it" moments as a mom include:

- Watching kids play Minecraft and hearing about every one of their buildings, structures, pets, and every other mundane detail of their Minecraft worlds.

- I once took my tween son to a Pokémon Go Fest. This heroic mom move required flights, a hotel stay, and two days of wandering around a park in not-ideal weather conditions. I was cold, confused, and surrounded by people who were passionate about something I knew nothing about.

- Acting extremely impressed when you must cheer on your kid doing a cannonball off the diving board for the one-hundredth time. Oh, if we only all had a nickel for every time we heard "watch me!" poolside. I mean, it would be nice if the kids could at least mix up their diving board water entry repertoire.

- Having to pretend I have a favorite Pokémon. Why it is important to my kids that I have a favorite one is beyond me. I'm a grown-up woman—I have a favorite snack, beverage, laundry detergent, and book. Pokémon doesn't really rank as a top priority.

- Taking teens and tweens to see their favorite YouTubers ranks high in the "boring things we do for our kids" category. I've attended several of these events and have no clue what was so impressive about some of them. But again, it seems on-brand that a middle-aged mother doesn't find them relatable.

Do you fake it till you make it or do you face it head on and go all in? Admittedly, in the early days at Mabel's Labels, we were big fake it until you make it fans. We pretended for a long time that we were not working out of a crummy basement. I distinctly remember hiding from my children in a dark closet, so I could have an uninterrupted meeting with a huge international parenting magazine about Mabel's Labels. I wanted them to think we were bigger than we were, thus discussion worthy.

Our early motto was to say yes to everything and figure it out later. Very Richard Branson style. On many occasions, in the early days, that worked out well for us. We needed to do those things to get ahead. Sure, it often meant staying up all night or lowering the standard of parenting. Baby not drinking bleach? Okay, we're good!

It was often chicken and egg stuff. If we turned up on *Oprah's Favorite Things*, could we handle the capacity? Hmm, not sure. But did we want to turn up on *Oprah's Favorite Things*? Absolutely! But we were not in a position financially to stock up on inventory and hire enough staff "just in case." As such, we did a lot of flying by the seat of our pants and calling in BIG favors from our friends and family when we needed to.

But as the business grew from baby to toddler to tween, we had to move on from faking it. The other thing that we realized was that as we were faking it, people actually loved our story of four moms in the basement building a label empire as their children puttered around them or napped. Your story is your brand. Other than realizing this, we also grew to learn that we were in a place where we had to face strategy, production, and growth head on. You eventually move from the "faking it" phase to the "they can sniff out a fake." We didn't want to be that company. We needed to make sure we had business plans in place to deal with whatever we had coming at us.

I have a sign in my office that serves as a healthy reminder of how to manage the full life of a mom and entrepreneur. People often told me, especially when my kids were young, that I had too much on my plate. As such, it seemed appropriate to have this mantra on my wall: "Don't tell me I'm burning the candle at both ends—get me some more wax!"

#bizhack

Faking it till you make it will only take you so far. Eventually, you'll get tired of playing charades, so be you from the start. Honest and transparent.

#lifehack

"Does this interaction leave behind a trail that I am proud of?" –Seth Godin

#momhack

What is a rule that you want to implement in your life? Give yourself permission to do it. Future YOU will thank you for it! It's okay to want time for YOU. You are still YOU, even if you're a mama at home and a boss at work.

chapter eleven

Surviving the Celebrations

Celebrations are a big deal in our household. March is the birthday month in my life—it brings birthdays for both me and Mabel's Labels, as well as one of my daughters.

I recently had a parent ask if I had any birthday party activity suggestions. Just thinking about the question exhausted me. I have hosted countless birthday parties. Actually, it's not countless: adding up my children's ages tells the story! It's no wonder I suffer from a bit of birthday party fatigue. Still, that doesn't mean the celebrations stop. We keep them coming, for every milestone, every birthday, and everything in between!

We've done it all: bowling, indoor playgrounds, parks, magicians, reptile guys, musical chairs, and the list goes on. Any way you slice it, at this point in my birthday party throwing career, the novelty has long worn off.

This can help you appreciate that six birthday parties a year is a big ask for someone who does not get inspired by Pinterest and has never baked a cake. Birthday party fatigue started kicking in years before my sixth child was born. Since then I have simplified things.

Here's my survival strategy:

- If I have the party at my house, I do not stress about the state of the place. It's only going to get trashed anyway. But what will the parents doing the drop-off think? Yeah, not really caring.

- No birthday presents. Guests are instructed that no presents or gift cards are allowed. I make it very clear on the invitation and people respect my request. One mother always brings me a bottle of wine. That, I accept.

- No loot bags. In return for not bringing my kid stuff they don't need, I refrain from giving our little guests junk too. The result: less going into the landfill and fewer sugar bugs on the teeth. I might chuck a little something at them by the door as a way to notify our friends that it's time to hit the road and avoid tears. Of course, there is one exception—the very cute Mabel's Labels Lootbag Combos!

- Birthday party timing is key. Book it for the 2:00 p.m.–4:00 p.m. time slot, which gets you off the hook for having to provide a proper meal. Get some cake and juice in their gobs, and your work is done!

Celebrations are great, but please don't ever feel pressured to host them in a Pinterest perfect fashion. Or do, if that is what makes you feel happy, makes you feel good. Don't forget to celebrate yourself as you celebrate your kiddos and other family members. We end up doing so much and celebrating so many people in our life that we sometimes fail to give ourselves that pat on the back.

At Mabel's Labels, celebrating everything is a big part of our culture. Our business birthday is in March and we party all month long. Along with doing fun activities at the office, we also have sales, promos, and events for our customers and with our online community. Because Mabel has been personified, when we turned sixteen, we had fun with Mabel getting her driver's license. Now that she is approaching drinking age, we will likely have some fun with that (shots with Mabel anyone?). For milestone Mabel birthdays, we have really done it up. When we turned ten, we hosted a big swanky event with all our longtime supporters and friends. We also took our entire staff team for an overnight away with a fancy dinner and day at some wineries.

Celebrations are important because they remind us of how far we have come. Often, we get caught up in the day-to-day operations and can lose sight of our wins. Celebrations also allow you to show thanks and be grateful for your team, customers, mentors, and family. It is also important that women entrepreneurs celebrate one another. If you ever have a chance to nominate someone for an award or invite them to speak at an event, do it!

We have won several national business awards, and because we are big fans of celebrating—we go all out! We organize limos for us and our staff, we wear ball gowns and drink champagne!

We must always support and elevate each other. One woman's success is every woman's success. I refuse to buy in or believe the stereotype that women are catty and cut each other down. That is just not my experience. Be supportive, and you will get support. Raise others, and they will raise you. Celebrate the women who are doing the tough slog of running businesses while raising babies.

HELL IN THE SKIES—BIG FAMILIES AND LONG FLIGHTS!

While this busy mama has to travel regularly with work, I've also had the daunting task of traveling extensively with many small children and for very long distances. Whether it's to visit family on the other side of the world or a shorter trip to a warm and sunny beach, traveling with kids comes with challenges. And when you have six kids . . . well, you can imagine how those challenges get multiplied along with the expense of all those plane tickets.

As the world slowly opens back up, and we get comfortable traveling again, some of us will be flying with extra passengers. There is a whole generation of new parents who have never been on a flight with their babies or toddlers before. And for others, their family has grown by a kid or two since they last traveled by air.

The thought of traveling with wee ones can be very daunting. As a mama who has traveled extensively with very small kiddos (and a lot of them at once, might I add), I'm hoping these bits of advice will help ease anxious parents!

One of my most memorable long flights with little ones was when we flew to Australia with our five children, the youngest being only five weeks old. It was celebration to see family and friends and introduce our growing brood to them, but first we had to make it through the twenty-four-hour flight (yes, twenty-four hours in the air with five kids under the age of six!).

Every time I fly alone, I relax and enjoy what I consider forced downtime. Whenever I hear a child cry or see a busy toddler walking up and down the aisle, I just sit back and remind myself to enjoy my flying time. Traveling can be stressful for families of all sizes, so you can appreciate the gravity of this undertaking for a family the size of mine.

The mayhem began at the airport with the inspection of passports times seven as the children played "dart around the line-up." Later, as we boarded the plane, I was greeted by the rows of passengers physically recoiling in their seats at the sight of us. Their facial expressions spoke volumes: "If there is a God, please make this hideous family walk straight past me and to the back of the plane."

But I have learned a few survival tips along the way. If you, too, want to avoid the urge to throw one of your children out of the airplane window, I suggest you take heed. The following are tips from when I traveled with my young kiddos:

Be prepared

Long before a flight date, I send a letter to the airline with my list of requests and expectations. It is a list that might be described as cheeky and demanding. I've included requests like bypassing lines and expecting airport assistance at all times. I communicate my child-sized meal requirements and inform them that the double stroller will be with us until we get to the gate. I ask that any issues with my requests be relayed to me by a certain date. And I bring a copy of the letter with me when we travel.

If you need a wheelchair, request one. On that long (long) flight, I was a few weeks post-surgery with my fifth C-section, and there were many privileges that went along with having that wheelchair.

If you have an infant, demand a skycot. There are never enough to go around and the squeaky wheel gets the grease, so get squeaking.

Book your seats strategically. In a row of three seats, we book the aisle and the window. Hopefully the middle seat remains unreserved, leaving you with the extra space to stretch out the little ones. If it does get booked, the passenger will normally happily trade with you.

If you are bringing a toddler along, bring a car seat. Strap it into the child's airplane seat to give them somewhere safe and comfortable to sit, eat, and sleep.

DON'T GET CAUGHT SHORT

Pack like someone is going to vomit or get the runs for the entire duration of the flight and you will be well prepared. For me, that means I pack clothes that will fit several of them. If I bring gender-neutral size 5 clothing, in a pinch most can wear them. Aside from dressing in layers, each child packs one spare outfit in a plastic freezer bag. Generic sizing allows for flexibility.

Hand out the pull-ups. A twenty-four-hour flight is no place for accidents. Even my toilet-trained preschoolers have to be pretty persuasive to get out of wearing a pull-up on a journey of that length.

Need help getting children to go to sleep? Learn your drugs and don't be afraid to use them—with the guidance of your friendly neighborhood pharmacist, of course!

Food and entertainment

Bring food. I don't think my children have ever eaten anything served on a plane, other than a piece of bread. Those "kid friendly" meals have a bit to be desired.

Invest in a handheld video game for older children. Gadgets are a mother's best friend on a long flight. For the smaller children, have a bag of tricks handy. Periodically pull out something new and entertaining like stickers or books.

Find yourself a young backpacker to help you on the flight. Slip the backpacker a few bucks and you've got someone who will happily play crazy eights and do color-by-numbers for hours.

My ultimate survival tip is to take a deep breath and remind yourself that at the end of it all, it's really only one long bad day. We can do anything if it's just one day, right? No matter how the flight unfolds, my experience is that I'll arrive at the baggage collection exhausted and emotional and be met by an angel. She's normally found in the form of an elderly woman who touches my arm and tells me that my children are gorgeous and so well behaved. I know she really means she considers herself lucky not to have been seated near us on the plane. But in the bleary, travel-aftermath, it's exactly what I need to hear.

#bizhack

When a friend of yours starts a business, gift them something that they would need for regular business use. This is especially helpful within the first few years of business. We give new parents gifts for the baby via baby showers, why not do the same for our friends when they start their new business?

#lifehack

"A life in hiding is a life unlived." My Grandma Lyons on living an authentic life.

#momhack

You are the expert of your family and the most qualified to make decisions for your family. Don't let anyone convince you otherwise.

chapter twelve

Helping Our Children with Autism Thrive

To any parent of a child who has had to navigate health challenges, I see you. This one is dedicated especially to my #autismmoms. I know how difficult those early days are when you first receive the diagnosis. You're trying to figure out how to be the parent they need, who can help them thrive and succeed despite their diagnosis. My son was diagnosed with autism when he had just turned three years old, and I had an eighteen-month-old and a newborn baby at home too. Although I was in a sleep-deprived foggy state, I vividly remember that time of diagnosis and trying to wrap my head around what it meant for our family.

Mostly it meant getting down to work and doing as much early intervention as possible. We set up an intensive therapy program, transforming our basement into a therapy center with a revolving door of therapists coming and going to work with our son. Money was tight and his program was expensive, but the gains my son made were immediate, and to this day, we consider it the best investment of our lives.

As parents, we had to commit to his growth and development. If you are a parent with a child with higher needs, commit to focusing on their development—whatever it is they need. It won't be easy, but it'll be worth it when you see them achieving and thriving and crossing certain milestones for themselves. For my number one boy, one key skill I wanted to focus on was organization, because we knew that would lead to further independence. I knew that the more work we did in the early years to make him independent, the better life would be for everyone as he got older. We implemented various strategies, and although we did this for our son, his five younger siblings have benefited from them as well. Here are a couple of things I focused on:

Make it visual. Children with autism respond very well to visual cues. When it comes to your child's daily routine, set them up with posters that have pictures of the steps they need to follow. Put up pictures of a child brushing their teeth or putting their coat on, for example. We put together a "Before School Plan," a visual chart listing all of their morning duties, which not only helped Mack but all of the kids start their day off right. If I saw a child standing in the middle of the kitchen with a "deer in the headlights" look, I didn't bark at what they should be doing, I referred them to their "Before School Plan." Training your kids toward independence is the best gift you can give yourself, and them.

Work with the school to keep kids organized. Often children with autism need assistance with executive functioning skills (things like managing time and attention, switching focus, planning and organizing). My kid is no exception. Ask your child's teachers to set up a reinforcement system to encourage these skills. As much as I'd like for my guy to be a math genius, if his executive functioning skills were better, all of our frustration levels would go down. As your child gets older, encourage them to use tools, like their agendas, to help stay organized. Labeling their gear will also help kids stay organized. It makes it easier for them to identify their school items and also teaches them stewardship over their belongings.

I am happy to report that my son is now a thriving university student. And while he still has moments of driving his mother crazy (forgetting his homework at school or misplacing his things), I'm taking this time to celebrate the amazing young man he is becoming.

He has anchored me, propelled me on a mission to keep all the world's parents and children organized—hello, Mabel's Labels—and reminds me that I can do hard things with great love and kindness. And so can you!

FIND YOUR COMMUNITY AND HOLD THEM CLOSE

In 2003, when Mack was diagnosed, parents were given virtually no information regarding treatment, resources, education, or help of any kind. It was pretty much a "yes, your son has autism . . . don't hit yourself with the door on the way out" kind of an approach.

I didn't even know where to get started. Keep in mind, this was long before social media. Finding help and connecting with other families was not a click away. Even in those early days, I learned quickly that my very best resource was other parents. I stand by that today. And with so many kids affected, there are more and more parents with experience that you can turn to. For example, if you are a parent digesting a new diagnosis, perhaps what I have learned will be helpful.

Connect with other parents. We are everywhere—schools, daycares, the internet. Other parents who have walked the path before you will share the best educational resources, help you learn to advocate for your child, tip you off about funding available, and generally UNDERSTAND how you feel.

Connect with other moms. You can find moms everywhere. School is a great place to start. If you can find moms with children on the spectrum who are attending the school your child will be attending, connect with them. They can give you the ins and outs of the special education resources available, how to negotiate support for your child, which teachers are best to deal with, and basically how to work the system in the best possible way for your child. Going to school is a big move for our kids (and us!) so connecting with school moms prior to school enrollment is key.

Find a support group. This is where I found my people. One night every month, I would meet with a group through Autism Ontario and I loved it. Sure, it is nice when a support group is there to hold your hand and let you have a little cry, but mine was all about action. We kept each other accountable and had each other report back about our goals for the month. THAT is my kind of support. Find a group that has the same goals as you do so you get the most out of it. Now that we have social media, you can find your people on the many Facebook groups out there. I wandered into a support group and truly found my people. But you have to find the right group. Some groups are for parents to share in their concerns and maybe have a little cry and get support that way. My support group suited me because we were a group about action. The facilitator was fierce—we were all there because we wanted the best outcomes for our kids, and we left with actual tasks to report back on at the next meeting. There was no "There, there, everything will be okay." And that was fine with me. Make sure your support group has the same goals as you do to get the most out of it.

Online groups. There are countless Facebook groups, Yahoo groups, and online communities. What I would have done for that resource all those years ago! These groups are a great place to ask questions, get answers, and have discussions. Find some you connect with and you have instant community.

Spend the money. Early intervention is important. Spend everything you have, because as much as we love our children, we all want them to leave our homes one day! If money is tight, be shameless about asking family and friends to contribute. I've seen families remortgage their homes. Do without trips and fancy things. Find as much funding as you can. We all want our kids to be taxpayers. Parents DO want to experience "empty nest syndrome." Pay now or pay later. Our children are our best investment.

Create a strong team. All of my extended family got trained in how to deliver therapy and how to follow our program. Yes, grandparents, aunts, and uncles were sent off for actual training. Cousins were involved in his therapy for doubles sessions. Everyone had required reading and knew what their goals were. Our monthly team meetings had many people around the table: parents, teachers, EAs, therapists, and his grandmother. Only the best team players were on our team.

Don't let your kid off the hook. Give your child with autism chores, hold them accountable, make them do what their siblings are doing, and hold the standards high. Don't "feel sorry" for your kid, otherwise you'll end up with a child with autism who is also spoiled. No one needs that.

I'm happy to report that my son's outcomes have been positive. He is in university, had the lead role in the high school play, has his driver's license, holds a black belt, qualified and worked as a lifeguard, volunteered in Africa for a summer, and is a loyal and loving friend, son, and brother. He has made many gains, but we still have him working with an Executive Functioning Coach. It is a long path, but a rewarding one.

CONNECTION DOESN'T HAVE TO BE COMPLICATED

Too often, in life, business, and love, we tend to overcomplicate things—how we relate and connect with each other, including with ourselves. What we say, where we go, who will we become. It can be something as simple as learning to talk to one another or enjoy each other's presence. An autism mom friend recently wrote a touching blog post about her son's desire for friendship, something that does not always come easily for "our guys." The response was amazing—with her loyal readers, fans, and friends honoring her request for prayers that her son's wish for friendship might come true.

It got me thinking about our own journey, and I suppose in lots of ways I took a very practical view of dealing with the friendship issue. Many of the positive results we saw came from expensive programs and relentless teaching. Here are a few of my tricks of the trade:

Birthday party invitations

Our guys generally don't get bogged down with invitations. When they get one, buy the birthday kid a ridiculously over-the-top present. Why? It might get your kid invited to more parties. Would it be for the wrong reasons? Who cares? I'm not above coughing up a great present in exchange for the amazing social opportunity a birthday party provides.

Birthday parties for our kids

Make them amazingly fun and invite lots of children. Create buzz by having "the" party to be at.

Be the fun mom

When I took my little guy to the park, I'd play chase with all the kids as the other moms sat and chatted over coffee. You see, all the park kids want to play with the fun grown-up, so being the fun mom creates social opportunities for your kid. While running around like a crazy lady, feel free to occasionally throw the stink eye in the direction of those coffee-drinking slackers who have no idea how lucky they are (wink!).

Teach your kid to be a good loser

When a kid has a major meltdown because he lost "What time is it, Mr. Wolf" at recess, he's not exactly positioning himself to make friends and influence people. No one wants to play with a sore loser. Teaching my guy to lose was a big part of his program. We made him lose board games over and over and practice saying, "Good game, would you like to play again?" without crying. Social skills programs and groups are great for tackling this common issue.

Autopsy the social event

After a social interaction or activity, be sure to examine the event with your kid. What went well? What could have gone better? Learn from the event.

Teach your kid not to be boring

Help them understand that we don't all want to hear about dinosaurs, the solar system, Pokémon, etc. Describe what someone's face looks like when they are bored or tuning out. Teach them that when they see that face, it's time to immediately change the subject to something the friend might be interested in.

Keep your kid cool

If all the kids are talking about Super Mario, get them a Super Mario game so they can be a part of the conversation. Dress your kid in cool clothes. If you have a kid who acts a bit nerdy, the last thing you want to do is dress them that way.

Self-stimulatory behavior (stims)

This is when you see the kids flapping, walking on tip toes, making a strange sound (verbal stim), or generally making an odd and repetitive movement or action. I spent a fair bit of time interrupting and redirecting stims.

Train their neurotypical friends

Teach them to be honest with our guys. It's okay to say, "Hey bud, don't stand that close to me when you're talking, okay? It makes people feel crowded." Or "Hey bud, we don't wear our ball caps that way once we are twelve years old, wear it like THIS." (And adjust their hat.) Neurotypical kids should be proactive, not merely observing the behavior—encourage them to chime in and share what they know!

Increase their social circles

If things are not going so well with the school friends, it's great to have other friends to rely on. My guy has friends from Scouts and sports as well. And let's not forget his besties—his siblings and cousins.

Teach, program, or do all of the above. Every kid deserves friends. Let's show them how to get some.

THINGS PEOPLE SAY

Ever heard someone say something out loud, though well intended, and asked yourself, *Why on earth would you say that?!* I know I have. Most of the time whenever people pass any comments or well-meaning sentiments, I know it comes from a good place. However, that doesn't mean I don't see red from time to time. The term "mama bear" aptly describes what happens to perfectly rational women once they become mothers—likening them to wild animals who will do whatever is required to protect their young.

This instinct is strengthened when something goes wrong with mama bear's cub. In the human world, it is particularly heightened for a woman who has suffered the loss of a child or finds herself the mother of a child with a disability.

For mothers who find themselves experiencing this firsthand, it seems an unwritten rule that people say the wrong thing. The very mamas you want to avoid saying the wrong thing to are the ones who hear them most often. While no one intends to be malicious or harmful, saying the wrong thing to mama bear can bite and will often leave her with no choice but to retaliate.

After experiencing a miscarriage, I was consoled with many inappropriate comments. The first was that I should feel lucky to have even fallen pregnant to begin with. The second comment referred to my miscarriage as "nature's way." Nature's way of what—ridding me of a child who didn't deserve to be born? It is never okay to tell a woman who lost her baby that it was a good thing.

I understand that being able to get pregnant is a gift and there are often medical reasons for a miscarriage, but for a woman who wanted *that* pregnancy and *that* baby, hurtful comments and well-meaning advice can wake mama bear from deep hibernation. For those who want to avoid being on her list of prey, I would suggest merely saying, "I am sorry for your loss." Full stop. That's it; that's it! Then drop off a casserole and offer to take her toddler for the morning. Understand that she is grieving and do not encourage her to "get on with it." Respect her grief.

A friend recently had a baby girl born with Down syndrome (DS). Between my son's autism diagnosis and her daughter's DS, we have heard it all. We both agree that once you have communicated the issue to people, there are two frustrating responses—they get the information all wrong or worse, they don't even bother to respond.

I wrote a very detailed letter explaining our family's new situation after my son was diagnosed. It included information about what treatment we were pursuing and how we were going to approach his autism. We forwarded it to all friends and family in hopes that we wouldn't have to repeat the painful story numerous times. One response indicated that our friend thought our son had Down syndrome. This told me that she must have merely skimmed over the letter or that she classifies all children with disabilities into one big heap. Either way, it was enough for mama bear to rear her ugly head.

Another acquaintance took the very wrong approach of explaining that she and I had "opposite" problems because her son was gifted. Last I checked, when diagnosing a child with autism, professionals do not consider "opposite of giftedness" to be a diagnostic criterion. There began her thirty minutes of quality time with me filling in all those autism knowledge gaps.

My friend recently had her newborn daughter out and about and someone actually asked her if the baby was "normal." The well-meaning stranger went on to say the baby was "cute anyway." Like I know this child and there is no "anyway" about it—she's downright adorable. At that moment, mama bear experienced the "flight" part of the "fight or flight" instinct. She felt a surge of panic and swiftly removed her child from the situation. It was only hours later when she reflected upon this encounter that her growl could be heard beyond the city limits.

There is another "compliment" that I hear occasionally—that I was given a child with special needs because I can handle it. As well-intentioned as that is, for a moment you feel like screaming (with a very sarcastic tone): "Lemme get this straight? I'm being rewarded for being a competent mother by having a child with disabilities." Doesn't really sound like a fair deal.

Not responding to the news of a family's situation is equally torturous. When such painful news is greeted with silence it is heartbreaking. While it's sometimes difficult to know what to say, take the time to figure it out. Saying nothing speaks volumes.

Some folks who are prone to foot-in-mouth syndrome might find a little reference guide of "do's and don'ts" to be a handy tool:

DO:

- Acknowledge the child has been born. Send a card and a present.
- If baby is well, ask to have a hold or cuddle.
- Speak positively about the child. Comment on her beautiful eyes or what a good climber he is.
- Offer help—drop off a meal, take an older sibling to the park.
- Take Mama's lead. If she brings up the subject, she is willing to talk about it.
- Educate yourself. Read and learn. It shows the family that you care and are interested.

DON'T:

- Generalize about the disability (e.g., not all children with DS are happy all the time; children with autism do not count cards in Vegas).
- Turn the news into gossip.
- Try to relate their situation to a situation of yours. You have not experienced this.
- Use outdated and offensive terms (e.g., the R word is inaccurate and inappropriate).

WHAT YOU CAN SAY TO A PARENT OF A CHILD WITH AUTISM

There are often discussions about what NOT to say to parents about their children with autism. I wrote about it myself—how some innocent questions and comments can actually be painful for a parent raising a child with autism. Although well meaning, some comments have the opposite of the intended effect. But please say something. Saying nothing can almost be worse. Someone recently asked me: What CAN someone say that is considered kind and helpful? That simple question stopped me in my tracks. Just asking it was a huge first step. I had a few simple suggestions that would go a long way with sensitive mamas. I've listed them below.

1) **Ask the mother if there are any resources or books you can read to learn more about autism.** That tells her you are interested in, and care about her child.

2) **Ask the mother if a playdate would be helpful and that you would be happy to host.** Our guys need social interaction and an opportunity to practice their social skills. Sadly, they are often the last ones to get invited for a playdate. Offering to host tells a mom that you're not afraid of her child and that you are open to fostering a friendship between the child with autism and her own child. Feel free to step it up and make sure to invite the child to your kiddo's birthday party. Those invitations can be rare occurrences as well.

3) **Compliment her child.** Mamas with kids on the spectrum seem to only hear the negative stuff. Many dread what they're going to read in the school agenda and worry that every time the phone rings it will be the school reporting yet another "incident." Like every mother, we want to hear that our kids are awesome, and it's nice for someone to notice. It doesn't have to be anything big. Here's some examples:

   - "I noticed your son's language is really coming along."
   - "Your daughter was really kind to my child today."
   - "I was volunteering in the class today and noticed your son sat really well in the circle!"

These are just a few simple suggestions that will make a tremendous difference in the life of moms of children with autism. Don't be afraid to talk to us. We're moms just like you, and like all moms, we love to talk about our kids—even (especially!) the ones with autism.

While we are generally sensible women of sound minds, discussions of our children can bring out our wild side. Be kind and thoughtful when you have a friend experiencing the loss of a child or one who has just received a "hard to hear" diagnosis. Remember, it's always easier to tame a bear with honey.

#bizhack

"Never allow anyone to be humiliated in your presence."
–Elie Wiesel

#lifehack

"If being around someone with a disability makes you feel uncomfortable, you aren't around someone with a disability enough." –Holland Bloorview Kids Rehabilitation Hospital

#momhack

What connects you to each other is your motherhood. Nurture that and each other.

chapter thirteen

Priceless Gifts of Learning

Life would truly be boring if we were all the same. We come in different shapes and colors and have different interests and likes, and I am thankful for that. I've always celebrated diversity and acceptance in my family, in my workplace, and in the world, in general.

I have a big extended family, and some are part of the LGBTQ+ community. As such, I've always felt comfortable knowing that some of my children might be too. And I am SO OKAY WITH THAT! I wanted my kids to know from the moment they were born that I felt that way. Love is love, and believe me, I have a lot of unconditional love for my kiddos!

The thought of my children hiding their sexuality or feeling like they would not be accepted in their own home is terrifying to me. When you look at the suicide rates within this youth population, I think parents are crazy not to make sure their kids KNOW they will be loved, regardless of who they love.

One way I created an environment of acceptance was to never make assumptions about my children's sexuality. I've always avoided gender stereotypes and would never say to my daughter "what boy do you have a crush on?" I always exclude gender from my nosey mama questions. I may bug my kids about telling me about their crushes, but I make no gender assumptions. In fact, I recently have been more sensitive that some teens may not have crushes at all—they may be asexual or just not there yet. So, I've even stopped assuming teens have crushes!

If they wanted to play with trucks instead of dolls, go for it! If they wanted to wear all pink or all black, I'm on board! I've always wanted to foster confidence in them so they could be happy in their own skin. The world isn't always easy, especially on kids today, so I made damn sure that they felt safe and secure in the knowledge that their family loved and accepted them. Full stop!

I've also recognized that growing up in a "traditional" family with one mother and one father didn't represent the many ways a family can be a family. I didn't want my kids to think that ours was "normal," which is one reason I love taking my kids to PRIDE events. They can see firsthand that families come in all shapes and sizes and are just as "normal." A family comes in many forms and is not defined by our experience of it. I love seeing my kids' eyes and minds open to the diverse families they see and meet at PRIDE.

PRIDE festivals are the perfect way of celebrating our family core values for my kiddos. And they're FUN! They are full of laughing, dancing, singing, and crazy fun activities and entertainment. The heteros could really take some lessons on how to throw a party!

LEARNING TO FAIL FORWARD

I was quoted in the Jessica Lahey's book *The Gift of Failure: How the Best Parents Learn to Let Go So Their Children Can Succeed.* The premise is that parents need to let their children experience failure so they can grow into resilient and self-reliant adults. At some point, every child doesn't make the team, gets cut from choir, doesn't have what it takes for the competitive dance troupe or cheer team. This disappointment will happen, and we've certainly experienced it in our household. I have been quite proud about how my kiddos have handled this kind disappointment, so I got to thinking what we've done that may have made our kids cope well in these very upsetting situations.

Role model great behavior. If you don't get a promotion at work, do your kids hear you complaining about the coworker in the office next to you who "stole" what should be your new job? Even worse, do you say to your kids, "I have no idea why you got cut when you're SO much better than Janey?" If you do this sort of thing, it's time to cut it out. Don't be that parent. Never bad mouth another child for being successful.

Show appreciation and be gracious. Even if your child didn't make the team, encourage them to send a note or email to the coach or league thanking them for the opportunity. When your child runs into friends who did make the team, remind them to congratulate them. This can be a difficult conversation, so practice with your child first. Role playing the first encounter after a disappointment can help your child maintain their sad emotions while celebrating a friend.

Let them cry it out, then move on. Being disappointed can be devastating, but it's also completely normal. Don't downplay it. They are entitled to those feelings. However, children need to be encouraged to also move on after an appropriate amount of time. Remind them of all the other activities going on in their lives and that they need to focus on those. Your child might appreciate working out a plan with you to increase their chances of making the team the next year. If your child got cut from a hockey team, perhaps enroll them in an extra power-skating class. They will feel empowered that there is a plan for improvement.

Not making the cut is disappointing for kids, but it is equally gut-wrenching for parents to watch their kids go through this, especially if you do believe that your kid should have made the team. Don't make the situation worse by letting your child think you are sad and disappointed. This is a time to teach perspective. This is a time for your child to readjust and consider Plan B. Try to look at the silver lining—learning to deal with disappointment is an incredible life skill. There will be many disappointments in life for your child, so use the opportunity to provide them with the tools to deal with it appropriately.

While "failure" is naturally upsetting, it happens in the business world as well. You know how once you are pregnant, you start noticing every baby? Thinking about getting a puppy and suddenly dogs are everywhere? This happened to me with small business. When we launched Mabel's Labels and I felt the emotional, financial, and physical energy it took to launch a start-up, I began noticing businesses everywhere. If I drove by a little shop that had gone out of business, I felt gutted for them. My empathy for business owners and entrepreneurs everywhere went into overdrive. Certainly, if a business is not going to succeed, it is ideal to fail fast. It's no surprise that people are serial entrepreneurs. It often takes the lessons from the first few failed businesses to finally find success in a business endeavor.

Failures within the business can also be disappointing, but we tried to always remind ourselves that "there are no failures, only lessons." A true failure would not be learning from mistakes and taking those with you into the next hire, project, or strategy. I think there is also a gift about knowing when to quit something. Quitting has a bad rap, and I get it. No one likes a quitter. We've been shamed for quitting, but sometimes it is the right thing to do. If I was still in the basement making labels all these years later, that would be a huge fail.

Entrepreneurs need to revisit their plans and goals; and sometimes if there is no path to success, moving on is the right thing to do.

I learned this lesson personally from my grandparents. They always knew when it was time to move on. They stopped driving at exactly the time they realized their age and reflexes made them unsafe. They stopped taking overseas trips when they knew that time of their life had passed. They never gave anything up too soon, and they never pushed it too far so that we were worried about their choices. They quit at exactly the right time and did it willingly and at peace with their decisions. It is a remarkable skill that I've found most people lack.

In both parenting and business, we can feel fatigue. My three oldest kids joke that I did a really great job raising them, but that I was a bit asleep at the wheel with the next three. Jokes aside, there certainly was a reprioritization of what really mattered, and I certainly chose wisely which hills I was willing to die on. Business fatigue is real as well. In both situations, it's important to ensure you are doing the things to keep you inspired, whether it is having a coach, therapist, mentor, exercising, binge-watching a comfort TV show, etc. Self-care takes many forms, and when fatigue sets in, it must be addressed.

Fatigue doesn't mean you're failing or it's a mark against your caliber as a person or your skills. It just means you are exhausted. And the only thing that will cure that fatigue is rest, and taking your foot off the pedal. Allow someone else to shine for a change while you rest and recharge. Too often, we make failure mean something about us when really, it's an indicator of where we need to realign and move forward. We think of failure as a bad thing, when in fact it can be the best thing to happen to us. If we don't fail, we don't innovate and create. If we don't create and innovate, we don't stay ahead of our game as pioneers and trailblazers in business. Apply the same philosophy to motherhood and life. Failure is a gift designed to show you where you can grow, build, and thrive. Allow it to be the gift you need.

#bizhack

Know when to let go of the day-to-day duties of running the business so you can concentrate on strategically growing the business. Get out there—read, talk to people, network, speak about your passion, and be a thought leader in your industry!

#lifehack

"You're as good as the rest of them, and better than none." –My Grandma Lyons, reminding us to be both confident and humble

#momhack

"A mother's job is to teach her children not to need her anymore. The hardest part of that job is accepting success." –An unknown empty nester

chapter fourteen

The Lasts of the Firsts

As a mom, I've experienced a lot of the last firsts. No more diapers, breastfeeding, first steps, or first day of school drop-offs.

The reality of change and transition can be difficult. Here is how I've survived my "last firsts," with kids.

Enjoy EVERY stage

I remember asking my mom once about her favorite stage of raising us. She said that she loved every unique stage for what each had to offer. She loved having four babies, loved having school-aged kids, and even loved having a houseful of hormonal teenagers. It was a great answer because it helped shape my perspective. Rather than lamenting the end of a particular stage, embrace the next. Don't get so stuck on one that you miss out on the others.

This too shall pass

Remember that each stage passes in the blink of an eye. You won't always have three kids in diapers or a baby up for a feed every two hours. I then went to six kids in hockey and spent most of my time sitting in cold arenas. I learned never to complain because I knew that in ten years I would be spending my Saturdays wishing I was sitting in an arena cheering on my little hockey players.

Know that it's not actually your last firsts

When I had my last baby, I told my mom that I was sad that I would never again have that feeling of falling in love with my baby as they came into my arms for the first time. She assured me that I absolutely would experience that feeling again. She said you get the same feeling of overwhelming, heart-bursting love when you are handed your grandchildren.

Don't lose yourself

Raising children is a full-time job, but eventually they are raised. Try to hold onto your interests and friends—or find new ones—while raising your kids. Carve out time to rediscover yourself. And please remember—you are a person too. You do not need to be the sacrificial lamb to be put on the altar of your children's happiness. Your happiness counts as well.

Have no regrets

We're all doing the best job we can. Don't dwell on what you could have done differently when they were younger. Remember you did the best you could at the time with what you knew. Then move on to do better in the next stage.

There are a lot of hard things about parenting, but perhaps the hardest part is that they go and grow up on us . . .

Tough transitions in life and business

I've often heard parents talk about difficulties their kids have with transitions. Sometimes it's a change in routine, a change in wardrobe, or a change in living situations. I've never had big issues with my kids and transitions. Even my child with autism didn't struggle too much in this department.

I used to think parents dealing with normal transitional stuff were exaggerating the difficulty of it, until of course, I had one myself.

It's not so much a change in routine that gets to him; it's mostly about clothing that can make seasonal changes quite dramatic. When spring would arrive, you would think he'd happily retire his bulky snow pants for the season. Not the case. While he would spend all weekend running around in shorts and a T-shirt, once Monday morning arrived, he was searching out his snow pants. Then there's his favorite winter hat. He would rather have his ears amputated due to frostbite than wear a different hat.

The funniest quirk had to do with his school uniform. He loved his school uniform and would happily wear it every day. However, when they had a special day when they could wear regular clothes, he refused to participate. On Valentine's Day, there was a school-wide competition to see which class wore the most red clothing. This is how the day played out:

- He refused to wear red and went to school in his uniform.
- He came home and reported that he was the only child not wearing red.
- He was furious that his class didn't win the contest for wearing the most red.

Yes, *he* was the reason his class didn't win, and yet it angered him.

When he turned five years old, he happily accepted and welcomed a party and presents. However, he was not prepared to give up on the age of four. When people asked him his age, his response was "*still* four," and we were only allowed to put four candles on his birthday cake.

Transitions are tough for kids, and they can be tough for adults. Let's put the CEO label on now to explore transitions within your business. At Mabel's Labels, one of our mantras has always been, "If you're not living on the edge, you're taking up too much space." Transitioning in life and in business can feel very much like living on the edge. You are peering over, not entirely sure what to expect.

Although there were changes and transitions made on the daily, there were three significant transitions that provided a lot of learning opportunities.

GROWTH

Growth is good! What company does not want to see growth? But with growth comes a lot of change. The biggest lesson I learned having a company that was growing quickly was to get comfortable being uncomfortable. The second we thought we knew what we were doing, something would happen that would make us have to learn again. I remember when we started having to hire staff and realized we had NO idea about Human Resources, how to hire someone, or what policies would make sense for our company. At that moment, one of the partners went to work, attended courses, and became our HR expert. That was also a time when we hired an HR consultant for her to work with.

Also with growth came the need for new equipment and tech; again, it's about learning and relearning what we needed to in order to support our growing business.

With growth also comes some tricky staffing questions. We always reminded ourselves about what we knew: "different horses for different courses," remembering that some team members were at their best during the start-up phase, while some found their sweet spot when we were mid-sized. All of that is okay! You need to get the right people on the bus and the wrong people off the bus, based on where your business is. Some of our staff loved the days in the basement as we made decisions with them over a cup of tea. Eventually, these decisions were being made around a boardroom table and without their direct input. That is what happens with growth. Some staff easily transitioned from start-up to a bigger more corporate environment, and some did not. Some had the skills of doing positions when we were in the start-up phase, then the company outgrew their skill set. Transitioning people as your company transitions is a reality, and it must be done for both the people involved and the health of your company.

Transitions can also be tough for entrepreneurs, who often find it difficult not to micromanage senior staff out of a desire to make sure they're doing things "right." Here's the thing: you bring in managers because you need them. You need their expertise, and you need to move on to doing other things in the business. The old expression, "If you spend your time working IN the business, no one is working ON the business." Sometimes you have to sit back and let your leadership team learn, make mistakes, and let the process happen. I'm not saying it is easy, but it is necessary. Besides which, micromanaging is not good for retention. No one wants to work in an environment where a control freak founder is putting them under a microscope constantly.

TRANSITION: GETTING YOUR PRODUCT FROM ONLINE INTO RETAIL

After many years of being an online and e-commerce business, we felt that we were missing a segment of our market that did not shop online. We worked hard to create a product for retail. One of the partners did an immeasurable amount of market research, speaking with retail experts, attending conferences, and traveling to see if this was a feasible next move for Mabel's Labels. In addition, we had already learned about the importance of hiring experts, so we did just that. Our retail consultant held our hand during the whole journey from idea conception to our product landing in big-box stores throughout Canada and the USA.

Mabel's Labels launched a product that was available in Walmart stores across Canada. For a small company that sold products exclusively online, moving into retail was a big step. We did our homework, including hiring a professional research firm to study the opportunity before pitching our product to Walmart buyers. Here are a few other lessons we learned along the way:

1) **No need to be intimidated**. While the world's largest retailer may seem intimidating, you have something of value to offer. Don't lose sight of that. Walmart's approach with small companies is much different from how they deal with the big multinationals. If you have a solid offer that fits their customer, they'll work along with you to make it successful.

2) **Know your prospective partner**. Walk the store, learn to speak their language, and understand their brand.

3) **Understand their customer**. Will the customer who shops at that retailer love your product? Does their customer look like your customer? Does your existing product and packaging need to be altered to appeal to the target consumer? Entering the retail market is a huge investment, and you don't want to see your product gathering dust on shelves.

4) **Be proud of your business**. You may be small, but big retailers are interested in the little guy. Your quirky beginnings and funny start-up stories are part of your charm. Don't feel like you have to hide them or be embarrassed.

5) **Be honest**. The due diligence and number of references a partnership will seek are extensive. Don't pretend to be something you're not. Practice honesty in business. Always.

6) **Bragging is allowed!** Go into your pitch loaded with customer testimonials, press hits, business awards, and other brag-worthy points.

7) **Practice your pitch**. Use your time wisely, be prepared, and stay on point. Buyers are extremely time crunched, so put your big selling stories up front; they'll find more time for you if they're interested in what you're saying.

8) **Don't know what you're doing? Get help!** Contract someone who knows about retail and has experience and connections. Ask all your friends involved in retail what and who they know. Remember, there is no such thing as a silly question.

9) **Be flexible and accept feedback.** Many buyers have extensive experience in the categories they manage. Be prepared to entertain changes they suggest, and always ensure you have resources available to take advantage of merchandising programs they may offer you. "All in" is fine in poker, but not at retail.

10) **Have all your ducks in a row**. If you get a "yes," then you'd better have a product to give your retailer. You need to understand all of your production, supply, distribution, and costing issues so that you can deliver on your promises.

Along with reaching a new market, other benefits of being in store was giving a brand impression on the shelf. People saw Mabel's Labels online, but now they saw our logo and product out there in the wild. It also allowed for PR opportunities. Moving into retail gave us something to talk about with the media, in articles, and on our social media channels.

TRANSITION: EXITING YOUR BUSINESS

People often ask us when they will know it's time to sell. For us, we were not necessarily thinking about selling, but being thirteen years into the business, we knew we had to pivot in some way to take our business to the next level. The four partners had taken the company to a certain level, but we considered perhaps hiring an outside CEO who could bring their wealth of experience to the organization. We were still operating as co-CEOs, which worked to that point, but we felt it was starting to be less effective for the organization. We also considered whether it was time to get outside investment in order for us to make some bold moves. Since we had always self-funded, this would have taken us out of our comfort zone, but it is always worth considering raising funds. We had not put it out to the universe that we were selling the business, and at that time, it was not our intention. However, we knew we had to do something.

In the midst of knowing this, we got a call from Avery Products Corporation, which is located in California but owned by Canadian company, CCL. They wanted to come in from Orange County to take us to dinner and have an introductory discussion. We thought there was no harm in attending dinner and having a chat. Our dinner discussion was productive and nothing they said turned us off, so we continued the discussion.

We had been previously approached but we didn't consider those other offers viable options for several reasons. The main reasons we were able to move forward with Avery included:

1) **The price.** We were able to negotiate the price that our company was worth and made sense to us. Remember, with four partners, the sale money was going to be divided, so everyone had to be on board with the number. Of course, because we had not planned to sell, the prior year had been an investment year. As such, when we ran the numbers for our selling price, they were lower than they should have been. If we had been gearing up to sell, we would have made sure we had a very healthy EBITDA (earnings before interest, taxes, depreciation, and amortization) margin, since that is what the price is generally based on. As such, the original offer was lower, but when we explained the discrepancy, the buyer understood and raised the price to what we had expected. They were going to profit from the investments we had made that year, and we wanted the price to reflect that.

2) **They loved our brand.** This was not a takeover; it was an add on. As such, we were still going to be Mabel's Labels. Avery loved our company for the brand and community we created.

They had no desire to take away the very thing that made us special. As such, we were going to remain our much loved brand, continue operations in our facility, carry on creating amazing products, and keep our incredible staff team on board. Other companies who expressed interest before were going to swallow us up, and that was not what we wanted.

3) **It's Avery labels!** This is the company best known for labels. It made sense from a product and culture perspective. Also, it meant we could tap into their professionals, procedures, and policies that would help make Mabel's Labels shine even brighter.

4) **They love and value what we've created and wanted to invest in it.** All the things we wanted to do to grow the company could happen, but with someone else's money!

EXIT PLANS—ARE THEY NECESSARY?

Even as a start-up, entrepreneurs should always be thinking ahead. Do you imagine your business will be a legacy business that you will leave to your children, or are you building to sell? The answer will determine how you manage and make decisions in your business.

Business planning and knowing where you want to be is essential. It was fine for us to be in a basement making labels in the middle of the night after we launched, but if we were still there ten years later, that would be a big problem. How much are you prepared to invest? And at what point do you start thinking about exiting?

HOW TO PREPARE BOTH PROFESSIONALLY AND PERSONALLY

As mentioned, our business was not exactly prepared because we had just done a big investment year. We had just scraped and revamped our very profitable fundraising program, and we'd invested significant funds into creating a new website and backend. This left our EBITDA lower than one would want it if preparing to sell. So, if you are thinking of selling your business do what you need to ensure a strong EBITDA margin.

Being prepared for a rigorous due diligence process is helpful. The buying company has the opportunity to look through every contract, partnership, and financial relationship during this time to ensure the seller is not hiding anything. No stone goes unturned. You want due diligence to go well so that the offered price for the company does not go down or terms do not get adjusted. Our housekeeping was in good order, and I've never been more thankful for an organized staff team. Everything got uploaded, and the Avery accountants and team inspected it all without issue. Due diligence can be a heavy and daunting process, so make a habit now of keeping great records so that it is less stressful when you go through it.

From a personal perspective, make sure you have a skilled and forward-thinking accountant. Ours had been with us since our business started, and we felt a strong personal relationship and responsibility toward all the partners. He had seen our business grow from the basement and felt a special connection with Mabel's Labels, often taking the role as business adviser as well. A few years before we sold, he ensured we set up trusts and holding companies so that if the time came that we were on the receiving end of a large sum, we could invest wisely and manage the tax situation effectively. This proactive approach was extremely helpful to each of us from a financial perspective.

TELLING YOUR TEAM: BUYOUTS CAN BE VERY DISRUPTIVE TO ORGANIZATIONS

We were very nervous sharing this information with the team because we didn't want to see them worried about their roles and the future of the company they loved. We actually hired a consultant who helped us craft the message in an effective way to help with the delivery. We decided who was saying what, and we rehearsed it. We had the additional complication that all through the buying process, we did not tell them. As a leadership team that valued transparency, this was very difficult for us. However, we did not have a choice. Because we were being bought by a publicly traded company, to share the negotiations and discussions would have been insider trading. The secrecy and dishonesty involved with our valued team felt awful.

We delivered the message to the group all together and explained what it meant. You could feel the relief in the room—they knew it was not a situation in which corporate robots were coming in and slashing our culture and killing our brand.

We assured them of our guiding principles during the process, including:

We would over-communicate with them. We would give them all the information as we got it. If we did not have an answer, we would find one.

If there was going to be a change, we would do it once and do it right.

In times of change and when we're nervous, it's time to turn TO each other and not ON each other.

The four partners ensured that we were visible in the office a lot following that discussion and gave everyone coffee shop gift cards and told them anytime they wanted one of us to go for a coffee to discuss the changes, we were there for them. Transitions in life, motherhood, or business are never easy. They can be turbulent or smooth—depending on how you choose to navigate them. What I've learned is the more we lean into our core values, the more we think of the big, hairy, scary, audacious goal and vision, the easier it is to transition into our next level growth. As long as you maintain open communication, have a plan in place to ensure nobody and nothing feels displaced, transitioning yourself as the business owner, and transitioning your team and overall growth, is something that will take place effortlessly. Remember, it takes effort to be effortless, so stay open, stay curious, and keep it growing (pun intended!).

CONCLUSION—EXIT, STAGE LEFT

Eventually, you are going to leave your business. That is just the reality. So many business owners are so busy growing the business, they are not thinking about what they eventually want to do with it. It's an important topic that is often not considered or thought about.

Why is it important to have some idea of your exit plan? If you are growing your business to sell it, you are going to manage it differently than if you plan on your children one day taking it over. If you are planning to sell eventually, you must realize that you will face due diligence, so keep your records in order.

After a business acquisition, there is often a requirement for the founder or founders to stay on for a certain amount of time to ensure a smooth transition. Once that time is up, it's important to evaluate if you are still your best self in that environment. So much change can happen; things change in leadership and operationally, and if you are not comfortable with the changes, your contributions may not be helpful. It's important to know when it's time to walk away and start your next adventure. Leaders must provide an inspiring and safe environment for their team. I've seen entrepreneurs stay on too long after the sale of their business, and it is not healthy for them or the organization. Sometimes quitting is for winners.

Be sure to prepare personally as well when there's a big transition within your business. You may have your accountant set up a holding company or trusts for your children. That is helpful if you have an influx of finances due to the sale of the business. Make sure you have an accountant who you trust. It is hard to think about exiting your business as you are just getting started, but remember you have to be thinking long term and strategically.

Over the years, some of my biggest lessons have been around my attitude. I certainly have had a lot on my plate. Between starting Mabel's Labels, raising six children, and working in the parenting space, there was never time to waste. I have found that my secret recipe for remaining productive and successful is to not take myself too seriously, to keep everything in perspective, to reject mom guilt, and to avoid complaining. Complaining and stressing over mom guilt are completely unproductive. If there is an issue or problem that makes me feel unsettled, I simply make a change. The only thing I can control in the chaos of my life is my attitude toward it!

We started Mabel's Labels to be able to make choices. We chose to live as ambitious business owners, loving mothers, and inspired women—a choice I have never regretted. And my hope is that if you decide to start a business, make a career move, or pivot your lifestyle entirely, may it be one that empowers, energizes, and enables you to live like a dynamic, enthusiastic, and fulfilled woman.

#bizhack

The secret sauce of a great business is a product or service that really does what it says it will, looks fabulous, makes life easier, and has genuinely passionate founders and staff behind it.

#lifehack

"Success is liking yourself, liking what you do, and liking how you do it." –Maya Angelou

#momhack

Transitions and change can be bittersweet for kids and for adults. Enjoy the present, but don't be scared of the future.

YGTMedia Co. is a blended boutique publishing house for mission-driven humans. We help seasoned and emerging authors "birth their brain babies" through a supportive and collaborative approach. Specializing in narrative nonfiction and adult and children's empowerment books, we believe that words can change the world, and we intend to do so one book at a time.

ygtmedia.co/publishing

@ygtmedia.company

@ygtmedia.co

Made in United States
North Haven, CT
26 June 2023

38259048R00147